To the memory of

Patrick Logan

— who would have enjoyed it

The Big Wind

Peter Carr

The White Row Press

The Big Wind

Peter Carr

The White Row Press

*First published 1991
by the White Row Press Ltd.
135 Cumberland Road, Dundonald
Belfast BT16 OBB*

*This book has received financial assistance
under the Cultural Traditions Programme*

*Cover: Joanna Mules
Text illustration: Geoffrey Fulton*

*Data transcription: Liz Rafferty
Typesetting: Island Publications
Printed by the Guernsey Press Company Limited*

A catalogue record for this book is available from the British Library

ISBN 1 870132 50 5

Contents

Introduction

1.	Oíche na Gaoíthe Móire	13
2.	The morning after	28
3.	'The vault of heaven their only roof'	41
4.	The journey into legend	46

Storm A—Z

Storm A—Z	63
Notes	125
Bibliography	132
Index	136

Preface

Books, like people perhaps, are conceived in all sorts of strange places. This one began with a chance meeting in the Main Street of Bangor, County Down; and my initial carefree involvement with it was as its publisher. However, after no less than *two* prospective authors had — I won't spare them — fallen by the wayside, it was left to me, now completely under its spell, to turn author and attempt to face *An Ghaoth* myself.

This book is in two parts. First comes the story of what happened on and followed after that awesome night, set, where possible, in the context of the folk beliefs of the time. Then comes a gazetteer of the storm's impact on the towns and villages of Ireland, in the form of verbatim extracts from contemporary newspapers.

Both parts are introductory. Many interesting issues relating to the Wind have, perforce, been left unexplored in this brief treatment. Nor is part two a definitive catalogue of the damage. Only a small percentage of this was ever recorded, and only a selection of that is reproduced here. However, it is important to include something of it, for there is probably no more eloquent expression of what the storm did to the fabric of the countryside or to peoples's lives than this simple litany.

Many thanks are due: to the staffs of the Linen Hall and Central Libraries in Belfast, the Ulster Folk and Transport Museum in Cultra, the Department of Irish Folklore, U.C.D., and the National Library of Ireland for putting up with me; to all the people who took the trouble to reply to my appeal for information (including the person who sent me a religious tract); to Leslie Clarkson, Derek Collins, Roy Johnston, Bill Maguire and Miceál Ross, for being generous with either their time or their specialist knowledge or both; to Ian Wilson for the idea, Robert Bell for the opportunity, and, moving out of rogue's gallery, to Cyril Collins for his imagination, and Donal O'Luanaigh of the National Library of Ireland, for his enlightened approach to the management of archive material.

1. Oíche na Gaoíthe Móire

The annals of Ireland do not furnish anything in the remotest degree parallel to this hurricane — nor has there ever been a visitation in this country attended with more tremendous, extensive, and calamitous consequences. *Dublin Evening Post*, January 8, 1839

The night of Sunday the sixth of January 1839 was a night of madness. On this night, the Twelfth Night, the night of Epiphany, Ireland was hit by what was perhaps the most cataclysmic storm to strike the country in the last six hundred years. It killed, maimed and ruined, threatening 'to sweep every obstacle before it from the centre of the earth'.[1]

No-one living could remember its like. The violence of the storm, its sheer brutality, horrified those who lived through it; many of whom counted it the most extraordinary experience of their lives. It was likened to a 'tornado' and a 'West Indian hurricane', and its magnitude was such that it was widely seen not as an extreme version of the normal but as a supernatural event. Along the western seaboard, people made their peace with God, convinced that the end of the world was at hand.[2]

The storm was also intellectually shocking. Like their counterparts in Britain and Europe, the country's intelligentsia had been dazzled by the recent advances in the natural and physical sciences, the expansion of knowledge in the fields of medicine, education, philosophy and exploration, and by the accelerating pace of technological change. Nothing seemed impossible. Theirs was an exciting and confident age.

With these changes came new ways of looking at things. In

particular, there had been something approaching a revolution in men and women's relationship with the natural world. Nature was no longer a bogeyman. In Ireland, wolves had been exterminated, the remains of the primal forest felled, vast areas of 'bog and waste' had been brought under the plough, roads, canals, and now railways were slicing the country into manageable portions and opening it to commerce, making the remotest fastnesses accessible. Wind and water had been tamed, and brought into service as sources of power. Indeed at sea, the invention of the steam engine threatened to make wind power obsolete. The old insecurities about the world were vanishing.[3] Nature it seemed, could be taken for granted.

Which is why the storm came as such a shock. In a moment of something close to primal chaos the fragility of the human achievement had been exposed. Every indication in the landscape that man was more than a brute beast — the cities and churches, factories and mansions — was humbled. Man was, very briefly, dethroned, and his self-confidence fleetingly, but deeply, shaken.

The timing of the storm was also seen as significant. Epiphany is a feast of revelation, the day Christ made his being known to the world. Within the Christian celebration, however, may be traced the faint outline of the older and perhaps darker pagan festival which it replaced. The night of Epiphany was associated with death divination.[4] It was a time when 'the living felt the dead very close'. As Lady Wilde wrote:

On Twelfth Night, the dead walk, and on every tile of the house a soul is sitting waiting for your prayers to take it out of purgatory.

Of course it is hard to find a day in the Irish calendar that does not have some dire connotation: but this mattered. Much was also read into the fact that it arrived on Sunday, reaching its height on Monday, the day which, in gaelic Ireland, is traditionally associated with the Day of Judgement.[5] All this enormously enhanced the metaphysical significance of the storm.

T he morning of Sunday the 6th of January began well. The sun rose at about half past eight on a land much of which was white from the previous evening's heavy snowfall.[6] The day was calm, so calm that two vessels which had set out from Cobh had to anchor 'as there was scarcely any wind'. The tranquility of the morning is remembered as being almost unearthly:

*Little Christmas morning. The children were out enjoying themselves
in the thick, fleecy snow which had fallen the night before.*

So appalling was the calm that the sensitive flame of a rush candle burned
in the open air without the faintest attempt to flicker, and so awe-inspiring
was the stillness that prevailed that voices in ordinary conversational
tones floated to and fro between farmhouses more than a mile apart.

As Thomas Russell of Westmeath put it:

there was something awful in the dark stillness of that winter day, for
there was no sunlight coming through the thick, motionless clouds that
hung over the earth.[7]

The children were excited. Not just because of the snow (that
was a bonus) or the ease and contentment that seemed to infuse
everything around them, but because it was Little Christmas, or
Nollaig na mBan, Women's Christmas. This was the day that had

15

been Christmas before the introduction of the Gregorian calendar, after which it had been commuted into a day of treats (if the budget ran to them), good food and celebration.[8] There would have been great activity in kitchens all over the country that morning, as the sweetmeats were baked, and the festive meal prepared. Everyone was looking forward to the evening's entertainments.

In the middle of the afternoon, however, it began to get close. It became unseasonably warm. Soon afterwards, in spite of a faint breeze, the heat became sickly. In Phoenix Park a 10°F rise in temperature was recorded. In Belfast the rise was even higher, and when Mrs Francis Howard, the wife of the Vicar of Swords, went to church that evening 'the night was very calm and hot, the air felt like air in a hothouse'.

It was all a bit odd, but not in itself alarming. In a house in Limerick it was noticed that the glass 'shewed the quicksilver under the extreme lowest mark of the barometer'.[9] This was an ominous sign, and one of the few indications of what was to follow. But such knowledge was exceptional. Almost no-one had the slightest inkling of the Odyssey that they were about to embark on.

For as Ireland, as all the Irelands, went blithely about their business, out in the eastern Atlantic, unknown to anyone, a deep depression was forming. Behind the warm front(s) which the country basked in that evening (and which party goers may have put down to the cheering effects of alcohol!), another bank of chill air was lurking. Much of the tornado-type activity that followed has been attributed to the swift change from warm to cold air.[10]

And then it happened. The storm began innocently, almost casually. Around nine o'clock a light westerly breeze sprang up, freshening 'to a degree that seemed to promise a rough night'. There followed a steady, relentless turning of the screw. As the *Dublin Evening Post* recorded:

about half past ten it rose into a high gale, which continued to increase in fury until after midnight, when it blew a most fearful and destructive tempest.

Elsewhere its arrival was sudden and explosive. In the little town of Kilbeggan in Westmeath:

There was at first a rumbling noise, like thunder, heard, which was followed by a rushing blast of wind, which swept across the town like a tornado, and shook the houses so much that the glass and delft were... thrown from the shelves.[11]

'Lord God have mercy.' People crowded in wherever they could, terrified for their lives. If their shelter was blown down, they would all move again, one woman having to go to three houses to give birth to her baby.

The effect was electric:

those who were in bed hastily jumped up and dressed themselves — many ran out of their houses into the fields and gardens, and in several instances where the inmates fled, the houses were soon after levelled to the ground.

What on earth was going on? Disquiet turned into consternation. In Limerick:

The watchmen took refuge in terror of their lives... no living creature being able to stand in the streets, while the spirit of the tempest was careering in all his might through the air, streaks of lightning at intervals illuminating the midnight darkness, and a shower of slates at every angle which was exposed to the blast, strewing the ground with broken particles, and flying before the tempest, we may add, like shreds of paper.

Towns and cities were plunged into darkness. People became frantic, their fears excited 'almost to madness'. Vast numbers deserted their houses, seeking shelter wherever they could find it. In Dublin crowds gathered in churches and under the Corinthian columns of the Bank of Ireland. Some were seen 'walking the roads where no houses were to avoid death'. In Drogheda:

Mr Clarke, one of the proprietors, very humanely had the underpart [of his factory] thrown open to the inhabitants of the densely-populated suburb in which it is situate, where immense numbers took refuge.[12]

Others stayed put, huddling together in whatever part of the house they judged to be the safest. Some slept through the whole thing, blissfully unaware that anything untoward had happened.

Often the wind came in gusts and 'blasts' (Galway was hit by 'whirlwind after whirlwind'[13]), in between which 'you could walk with a lighted candle in your hand'. Then the fearful rumble started again:

you could see the frightened faces of the women and children when they heard the ever increasing roar of each gust as it rushed towards us at a distance. And when the crash came the house rocked and quaked, so that several times we thought it would come down.[14]

It was like being in a bowling alley in the position of the skittle. Where the wind was continuous, powerful currents and eddies were reported.[15] In Dublin the wind would rake the street first one way then the other, and when contrary blasts met a whirlwind formed, which made the stoutest houses 'tremble and rock to their foundations'.[16]

This rocking of houses was experienced all over the country. John O'Donovan, in the Wicklow mountains for the Ordnance Survey, wrote of his hostel rocking beneath him 'as if it were a ship',[17] and in Portadown, the houses 'groaned like a vessel at sea', the beds and furniture being 'visibly agitated'. This was more than many places could take. In Sligo good houses were 'shivered to atoms'. Hundreds of well made buildings collapsed, and many more

*'From 11 o'clock at night until 5 o'clock this morning the street
presented the appearance of two invisible armies throwing slates,
pots, and tiles at each other... with such violence as to shatter
them into bits.'*

subsequently had to be demolished.

Roofs suffered particularly badly. Slated roofs were plucked
clean like Christmas turkeys, the back roof of the barrack at
Longford disappearing 'as if an explosion of gunpowder has taken
place inside'.[18] In Carrickfergus sheeted lead roofing was 'rolled
up like an ancient scroll'.[19] Once the roof had gone the room's
contents were fair game:

beds, palliasses, pillow cases, and other bed-room articles [being] carried
on high... like so many feathers[20]

Many houses, totally traumatised by the experience, gave up and
committed hari-kari. This involved the chimney-stack (often built
on a monumental scale) coming down through the roof, and perhaps
on through the house, carrying all before it. Lady Mountjoy's 'fine
mansion' in Rutland Square was greatly injured in this way; and in
Clare Street another stack 'destroyed a female'. (Gentlefolk died,
females and servants tended to get 'destroyed'.)

Staying indoors was a high-risk activity. But then so was going out. Anyone who went outside risked being 'blown about like a ball'.[21] In Dublin people had to creep across O'Connell Bridge. In Belfast a man and a child were splashed against a wall and killed, in Kilbeggan a policeman was scooped up then dashed to the ground, and left throwing up blood.[22]

The storm reached its height between two and five a.m., presiding unchallenged over Ireland. The accounts of this phase have a surreal quality. Streets became 'impassable'. People 'standing together' had to resort to signs in order to communicate.[23] Slates, stones and the contents of kitchens and bedrooms performed a *danse macabre* in the air, to the accompaniment of howling, screaming and sobbing, and the 'incessant' tinkle of glass. Every so often fugitive figures, many of them naked, flitted past seeking safety. The scene was worthy of Dante.

This level of anarchy was not confined to the big towns and cities. The one-street village of Bruff, in County Limerick, seemed to have been invested by:

two invisible armies throwing slates, pots, and tiles at each other, as, when the wind shifted it would bring the slates from the opposite side against the slates at this side, and they often met in the air with such violence as to shatter them all to bits.[24]

In some parts this activity was accompanied by a spectacular *Son et Lumière*. Lightning struck the south-west,[25] and in Dublin, according to the usually reliable *Evening Post*, the *aurora borealis* burned brightly 'mantling the hemisphere with sheets of red'.[26] Some found time for aesthetic contemplation. This was not begrudged. There was a beauty in the horror. People realised the uniqueness of what they were living through. Between panic attacks, the correspondent of the *Kilkenny Journal* found the whole thing 'awfully sublime'. The storm accorded perfectly with the Romantic idea of the beautiful, and the reportage is full of gushing references to its majesty and grandeur.[27]

The fireworks, alas, were not entirely celestial. In the Bethesda Chapel in Dublin, where earlier in the day grateful worshippers had given thanks for its deliverance from a fire on Saturday, the embers re-ignited, burning the church, its school, six fine town houses, not forgetting the attendant 'House of Refuge for reclaimed

Chimneys falling, fires raging, people running hither and thither...

females' to the ground. This 'inferno' was in itself a Grade A disaster, which severely tested the city's fire-fighting powers. Pieces of burning wood were carried far across the metropolis, and it was feared, recalling the Great Fire of London, that the blaze might be fanned 'into a general conflagration'.[28] In Kilbeggan:

the roof of a thatched house... fell in and caught fire... and in a few moments the whole range was on fire. The scene that followed was terrific beyond description. The inhabitants fled, some of them naked, into the fields, leaving all their little property behind. In less than an hour twelve houses... were consumed.[29]

Over a hundred houses were gutted in Athlone; and eighty-nine in Loughrea, which had another thirty levelled by the wind, and others damaged, leaving six hundred homeless. In Moate, where sixty-three houses burned down:

it was said you could pick pins in the yards of houses in the townland of Gurteen, about two miles south of the town, so great was the light from the burning houses.[30]

Along the Tyrone-Monaghan border 'there was a fire in every townland'.[31] In places the sparks were so thick that flames seemed to 'fall from the clouds'.[32] People were blinded by airborne cinders. The tragedy is that these wounds were largely self-inflicted. Few people thought to put out the kitchen fire. Fires were set as usual that night (by being smothered in enough ash to see them through to morning), so when houses were opened, these dormant mounds became little volcanoes, the sods and coals 'dancing on the hearth'.[33] In the circumstances, having the roof blown clean away was almost a blessing, for it could save the house from fire.

The authorities, such as they were (the police force had only just been formed) did their best, but their resources were quite unequal to the problem, and while the police and military were to the fore in fire-fighting in Dublin, elsewhere, in spite of the presence of policemen, the citizenry often took the lead.[34]

Elsewhere, the problem was not fire but water. In Dublin the Liffey overflowed the quays,[35] and on the waterfront in Limerick:

when the affrighted families hurried from their beds to the vaults below for protection, they were repulsed in despair by the rush of water from the inflowing tide, raised to an unusual height by the force of its kindred element.[36]

On the west coast of Galway (which always goes one better!) the risen tide left the dunes and beaches squirming with herring, cod and congers. High tide came between 10 and 11 p.m., and it is lucky that it did not come later.

As well as the spectacular tide, parts of the country were visited by bursts of torrential rain. Thomas Russell records that:

There is another curious and undoubted fact relating to the great storm; it is that showers of salt water fell in many places. I have heard this stated by many persons, and among them one of my own brothers. The showers would never last but a few seconds, and resembled small waterspouts more than showers. They fell in such torrents that one was wet through almost instantaneously by them, and in these douches some of the water

'Hickey, his wife and both children were... carried off by the flood.'

was sure to reach the mouth.

And, as if this was not enough, the temperature rise of the early evening had produced a sudden thaw. These factors combined to put the drainage system under considerable stress. We get a hint of just how much from Tullamore, where the flow of the usually gentle Brosna broke a huge metal waterwheel. In the towns nothing drained properly as the pipes were stopped and the water spouts 'riven from their fastenings'[37] There were flash floods in Strabane. The Grand Canal and the Shannon burst their banks, flooding 'vast' areas of country:

At Coonagh a poor man of the name of Hickey, his wife and both children

were... carried off by the flood. The father and both children perished —
the mother is thrown upon a hedge, and is left a desolate widow.[38]

Though the towns had it bad, it is to the countryside that we
must look for the archetypal experience of the storm. In the
townlands the 'tempest' took nearly everyone completely by
surprise. In spite of the elaborate weather lore of the country, no-
one had managed to predict it, a fact which greatly miffed many
rural forecasters.

People tried to secure their homes. Windows were blocked,
sacks of corn piled against kitchen doors. It was vital to keep these
in place, for they were the first and often the only line of defence,
and if either went the roof could follow. Staying put, defending
the house, took courage. As O'Donovan recalled:

About two o'clock the storm became so furious that I jumped up,
determined to make my way out; but I was no sooner out of bed, than the
window was dashed in upon the floor, and after it a squall mighty as a
thunderbolt.[39]

Somehow, he managed to close the shutter, however the next blast
stoved it and threw him aside:

I closed the shutter again despite the wind, and kept it closed for an hour,
when I was as cold as ice (being naked all the time).[40]

But help was to hand, and when his colleague returned with the
owner, who had been out trying to pacify and protect his cattle, the
shutter was jammed closed and the roof was saved.

O'Donovan had four sound walls around him. Not everyone was
so fortunate. Though many houses were then stone-built, a majority
of dwellings were constructed from sods and mud (and built with
the fairy equivalent of planning permission.[41]) Many cabins were
gerry-built, badly roofed 'garrisons for rats',[42] houses that 'you
wouldn't put pigs in today'.[43] Most were thatched, the thatch simply
resting on the eves, anchored by its own weight. As few houses
had side windows, and maybe only a small back one, the house
was most vulnerable to a frontal assault, and west facing houses
fared notably poorly.

For the people who lived in these houses, the struggle was often
hopeless. People were left to cower in the corner as their dwellings
crumbled about them:

The storm became so ferocious people thought
the end of the world was at hand.

The houses were shaken to the very foundations, plaster fell from the walls, rafters creaked, and stout beams groaned under the terrific pressure.

Roofs collapsed or disappeared. One in Westmeath travelled from Kippenduff to Keel, the next townland; another in County Leitrim sailed serenely across Fenagh Lough.[44] Hill farms in eastern Clare were 'bowled... down the mountains'.[45]

people couldn't stay in their houses... they were falling down on top of them. They went out to the fields, and they were lying down with their arms round rush-bushes to save themselves from being blown away... They crawled over to the rush-bushes. If they stood up straight they'd be swept off their feet. Many a one was knocked down when they tried to walk.[46]

In County Monaghan:

those who took courage and volunteered to assist their neighbours had to travel on all fours. They were obliged to embrace each other and shout at the top of their voice to make themselves heard.[47]

Some were drowned by being blown into dykes and bog-holes. In Leitrim, in the shadow of the Iron Mountains, folk abandoned their houses and took refuge in the 'Alths'. Where did you hide when the places of shelter were all prime targets? In Moate a man got into a barrel for his own safety and was blown around the town. People hid behind hedges and ditches, and where they had neighbours, crowded into the houses that were still standing.

Several children were literally blown away, and never seen alive again. Thomas Heaney got through by being kept under a pot.

Sometimes even these would go, and everyone would have to move again, one woman in Doocastle, having to 'go to the third house to have her baby'.[48] Martin 'Junior' Crehan, the well-known Clare fiddler, tells the story that after his great-grandmother's home had been ruined, she and her dozen children (the baby in an apron) sought shelter in the only house in the village left intact. She found it full to bursting, and was afraid that she would be left outside when someone piped up:

'Make way for the mother hen and her twelve chicks!'[49]

Young children were particularly vulnerable to the menaces of the storm, so wherever possible, they were consigned to places of safety. In Giviteen little Thomas Heaney was 'put under a big pot', and near Mohill in County Leitrim young children were 'put into oak chests and stones put on top of them to save them' (which must have been every bit as scary as the storm!).[50]

But never mind the childer, what about the bastes? Farm animals and wildlife had a very rough time. As so often, however, the detail (and, probably, the scale of the slaughter) is unknown to us. Like the rural poor, animals tended to feature only marginally and in a generalised way in accounts of the storm; and unlike them, their descendents have not been cornered in their lairs and burrows by folklorists politely seeking to tape their recollections.

The little that there is about birds and animals makes dispiriting reading, with pigs roasted alive and cattle maimed and killed in their byres. Mercy killings will have put meat on many tables in the days that followed. Stones 'dug out of the hills' killed innumerable sheep, one Clare farmer reportedly losing 170. Near

Newbliss in County Monaghan:

The hens were blown out of the bushes and trees where they used to roost and most of them were never seen again.

Others got caught in gates and fencing and had their plumage stripped, and from County Leitrim there is a record of roosting hens being blown to a distance of half a mile, which must have been a great offence to their dignity.[51] There was a massive cull of wild birds. In Galway a pile of dead seabirds was found at the base of Ceann Reanmhair.[52] They had been grated against the cliff like bits of cheese. At Newgrove in County Limerick:

the noisy inhabitants of the rookery strewed the ground in thousands

and in parts of County Monaghan the ground was reportedly 'black' with the mangled bodies of crows, which species became 'nearly extinct' in the county for years after.[53]

Ricks went disco-dancing over the fields.[54] Heaps of turf took wings and flew.[55] Stacks of hay and oats, many of which were bigger and more soundly built than the average cabin,[56] were fretted to pieces or carried off *en bloc*. In Clough, County Antrim, one haystack was driven against a hedge and blown through straw by straw, the hay 'sticking out like needles' on the far side of the

There was an appalling slaughter of birds, and a destruction of nesting places. Crows became almost extinct in Roscommon.

hedge.[57] The crops were heading back into the fields — or beyond. Sheaves of oats reportedly glided across the mouth of Strangford Lough, touching down near Portaferry.[58] At Island Magee:

stacks of different sorts of grain [were] wholly swept into the sea.

There was no peace even for the dead. Near Blarney:

a house in which a corpse was waking was blown over, the persons present having only time to get outside the door when it fell.[59]

They did well, in Athlone 'part of the corpse was consumed [by fire] before it could be dragged out'. At Ballylesson, near Belfast:

two coffins... were actually exhumed from their graves by the uprooting of two adjacent trees![60]

2. The morning after

Monday morning, first light. Out in the Cavan countryside, a six year old girl wakens to find daylight streaming in through the roof of her father's cabin. What was going on? Over in Ross in County Galway, the Martin family emerge from the cellars of their mansion to see nothing between them and the sky. Was it all a bad dream? Were they still sleeping? Unfortunately, they were not.

That morning the sun rose on a chastened, wasted Ireland. Familiar things had become unrecognisable. Well-known landmarks had gone. Even the clouds, according to one, still dazed correspondent, seemed to present a 'singular, awful, and brassy' appearance.[61]

The country came to a standstill. People were dazed and bleary from a combination of sleeplessness and nervous exhaustion. In the towns, shops were shut 'as if death had visited the inmates of each,' but the streets were crowded. People promenaded, gawped and gabbled, the storm being the 'sole engrossing topic of conversation'.[62] Mrs Francis Howard was out smartly after breakfast:

every person we see tells us of new horrors... all had stories to tell of suffering and providential escapes[63]

It was all too delicious. For days afterwards, she found herself unable to 'listen or think of anything but the Storm.' She was giddy with it, drunk with it — as was everyone around her. People talked the horror out of their systems, neutralising it, shedding it in routine. This process was necessary and cathartic, and through it the uncertainty, the distrust of nature died away. Normality made a comeback.

However, the elation of having survived was soon overtaken by the grim business of reckoning up the damage.

The storm had been an ecological disaster, an Irish Chernobyl. Dublin resembled 'a sacked city'. Belfast looked as if it 'had been reduced by artillery'. The countryside appeared to have been 'swept clean by a great broom'.[64] Its appearance shocked travellers. One man who journeyed from Carrickmacross to Newry reported that:

on the whole line of the road, a distance of twenty-two or twenty-three miles, he did not see more than three or four standing stacks of grain.[65]

Another, who had been out in Donegal, found 'the face of the country... a continual wreck.'[66] Everywhere its aspect had been changed from that of plenty 'to that of woe and want.'[67]

The seats of the nobility and gentry had been savaged. Hundreds of country houses were damaged. At least half a dozen had to be abandoned. Stately demesnes lay in tatters, their trees uprooted or 'snapped in pieces like glass'.[68]

On the estate of the Earl of Granard near Longford groves of 'noble beech trees' were mown down 'like... corn'; while ash and fir were 'hurled over the demesne wall as if discharged from an engine'.[69] At Seaforde, in County Down about 60,000 trees were lost, and at Garbally Park near Ballinasloe, the Earl of Clancarty was left 'almost without a tree standing'.[70] Joyce writes that:

A gentleman living in the County Mayo had at that time an extensive well-wooded estate verging on the Atlantic. That night 70,000 of his trees were blown down; so that, as he expressed himself to Dr. Petrie — who told me the story in Dublin many years afterwards — "my entire estate is now as bare as the palm of my hand".[71]

In places it was easier to say what was left than what had gone. Such woods as survived had 'big gaps cut through them', as if blasted with grapeshot.[72] Much beautiful and ingenious landscaping

The dead rising.
Not content to torment
the living, the storm
sought out the dead.

was destroyed, and immense botanical damage done. The splendid avenue of elms in Phoenix Park was levelled, and near Longford:

The dark entrance avenue leading from Newtown Forbes, which seldom failed to impress the visitor with feelings of solemnity and awe, and which seemed so suitable an approach to the mansion of an ancient family descended from a line of kings, is now completely spoiled and laid bare.[73]

The loss touched different people in different ways. Philistine owners, or perhaps correspondents, called their trees timber and reported the damage in terms of its sterling value. Others felt the absence of every tree:

in what ever direction one turns, a person cannot walk two yards without missing an old and valued friend[74]

Thomas Lefroy, later Chief Justice of Ireland, wrote to his wife of the 'anguish' he felt at the loss of his woods; and on Carraun Hill near Athlone an inscribed stone was erected commemorating the loss of the 'FINE OLD TIMBER' on the Waterston demesne.[75]

30

Even war heroes don't always qualify for this sort of treatment. Why did the ruin of their demesnes touch the gentry so deeply?

To answer this we must seek to enter the minds of the nineteenth century gentry. Trees were then very much in vogue. This was the golden age of private planting.[76] Captive, ornamental trees were devotional objects, the wooded demesne being seen as one of the landscape's chief embellishments. Like the presidential retinue or the smoked glass in the Lincoln Continental, they protected privacy and announced importance.

Trees had become not an index of wildness, but of civilisation. They denoted islands of culture, taste, accomplishment, in a barbarous, superstitious landscape — nowhere more so than in Ireland, where they were fast becoming the only objects in the whole distracted countryside that landlords felt they could trust. They did other jobs too, they insulated the landed from the miseries of the countryside around them; they implied long occupation, and through that legitimacy of ownership. So in a curious way, the removal of trees challenged the authority of the landed classes. (One of the most distressing features of the damage done at Newtown Forbes was that the venerable old mansion could henceforth be seen from the road!)

Now their magnificent groves and arboretums were just so much lumber, to be offloaded on a collapsing market. In Dublin:

no timber merchant would go ten miles out of the city to buy a tree — and he would not, just now, take a present of 1,000, twenty miles from Dublin... There is a glut — and these beautiful trees are now nearly valueless[77]

It was thought that it would take a generation to restore the countryside to the luxuriance that it had enjoyed the summer before.[78] What remained presented a bizarre appearance, with:

trees, bushes and hedges bent or lying level: the road was swept dry; and as for the stacks of hay and corn and the ricks of turf they were nowhere to be seen — all blown off into space. The very grass of the fields was lying flat as if cowed and frightened.[79]

Salt was tasted off trees forty miles from the sea.[80] In Roscommon walls and gates had 'a salty crust'.[81] Seaweed was found on hilltops.[82] Herrings were picked up six miles inland.[83] Stormy petrels 'were found dead everywhere in the middle of the country'.[84]

Fish found high in the hills around Lough Sur were gathered up and salted.[85]

The Shannon and the Boyne became so thick with hay and oats that it seemed as if they might be walked across.[86] Lesser rivers gagged, flooding the countryside around them.[87] In Corraslira a lake was 'taken', and hundreds of perch scattered over the fields.[88] In County Down, the crannog on Ballyrony Lough was 'shipwrecked' and blown on shore;[89] and near Kanturk, in County Cork:

three acres of the Bog of Glounamuckalough... moved completely from its position and after traversing a distance of a mile, and crossing a rapid river, landed on the opposite side.[90]

Nothing was where it should be. The produce of the land was in the rivers, and the rivers were in the fields. Boats were put out to gather hay. Much of the harvest ended up in the Atlantic and the waters of the Irish Sea. More was swept into 'old scraws and bog holes', or caught up in hedges and the branches of trees.[91] Grain was killed by frost and eaten by birds, or grew up where it fell:

Hay and oats were sometimes mixed together, and it was no easy job to separate them... no man could tell what was his own.[92]

People got 'as busy as bees in a hive', retrieving the grain in 'horse's carts and donkey's carts and creels and in bundles on their backs'. However, a lot was never seen again:[93]

Farm implements, too, in some cases, joined in the general dispersal, and were never afterwards recovered.

For some, it was all too much. More than seventy years after that extraordinary morning, the great gaelic scholar and lexicographer P.W. Joyce recalled one of his neighbours, a prosperous farmer, staring bitterly into his empty haggard:

Suddenly he raised his two hands — palms open — high over his head, and looking up at the sky, he cried out in the bitterness of his heart, in a voice that was heard all over the village: "Oh, God Almighty, what did I ever do to You that You should thrate me in that way!" The little group of people were struck dumb with awe; and as for me, though little more than a child... I was so frightened that I turned round without a word and ran straight home.[94]

People survived by helping each other. There was an outbreak of something close to brotherly love. Folk opened their houses,

Trees, what trees? The demesnes of Ireland were savaged, the great country houses left naked to the gaze.

sheltering, and where necessary, feeding and clothing relatives and neighbours. As Mary Kettle of County Cavan recalled:

it was a very curious thing the day after the storm to see families carrying their beds and bedding and stools and pots and pans to their neighbour's houses.[95]

This warmth, a coming together in adversity, was so universal that it is almost shocking to read of a clergyman in County Cork who *took refuge in a hotel.* Had he no friends or neighbours? Did no-one love him?

The appearance of this Dunkirk-like spirit led many to remember the days following the Wind as a time of cheerfulness and good-

'People got as busy as bees in a hive.' For some, though, the storm was the last straw. Unable to afford to fix their houses, they took to rough shelters made of sods.

humour. It was also noted with approval by several newspapers, amongst them the *Ulster Times*, which, missing the point somewhat, declared:

How angel-like is this! How beautifully demonstrative of the blessed superiority of the Protestantism which is the glory of our North![96]

However not everyone was on their best behaviour. 'In defiance of the law' men and women invaded a demesne near Shinrone, County Offaly, cut up the fallen timber and sold it 'openly' in Nenagh and Roscrea.[97] But was this an outrage or a bold throwing off of the shackles?

There was also looting in Loughrea, where 'wretches... forgetting they were... Christians' robbed storm victims, several being arrested in possession of 'bacon from the house of an industrious man'. But was this looting or class warfare? The 'industrious classes' were mainly farmers, some of them sub-landlords, who were doing quite well out of the system. Their persecutors?

I am glad to say they are not Loughrea men; they are a nest of vagabonds called thimblemen, *who lately came here*, and are spread over the town.[98]

These were the disaffected and dispossessed, in from the country without skills or prospects, organised into loose societies, and militant in a time of recession and unemployment. It was a hint of what many feared was to come.

But this was strictly a minority activity. Most people's energies went into making their houses weather-proof. This was hard, bitter January; and in case anyone needed reminded of the fact, there was a heavy snowfall that evening. The weather remained 'exceedingly unsettled'. People stayed jittery, and on several occasions during the following week a second instalment was feared, the appearance of the *aurora borealis* in the middle of the month doing nothing to dampen apprehensions.[99]

As the picture clarified, it became clear that all had not suffered equally. Ulster, the west and the midlands appeared to have borne the brunt of the storm. In Dublin, though 'vast damage' was done to the Liberties, the main civic and public buildings had come through the storm well, Dublin Castle and the Viceregal mansion, remaining largely unruffled. (Just whose side was God on?) The press view was that the capital had got off lightly, given 'the fury... with which it was assailed'.[100] Dundalk, however, had been 'fearfully' damaged, and Drogheda was pronounced 'a complete wreck'.

Almost every class of building had suffered. Church steeples had been felled, antiquities and follies scattered, factories and barracks ruined, windmills decapitated and set on fire.[101]

Agriculture, industry, commerce and communications were all seriously disrupted, nowhere more so than in Belfast, where the town's great cathedrals of manufacture were hard hit, the 'large and beautiful new weaving factory... opposite the Lunatic Asylum' coming down, as did the 184' chimney of Mulholland's flax mill,

They clothed and sheltered friends and neighbours.
There was an outbreak of brotherly love.

most handsome specimen of masonry in the North of Ireland'.[102]
Five of the town's biggest smokestacks fell (which will have done
the air quality no harm at all). Belfast would not again suffer such
damage until the blitz of 1941.

The mess was even worse in the 'suburbs', the slums and shanty
towns that existed around the then inhabited town centres. Here,
the hovels of the poor were 'blown to atoms'.[103] The homeless
suffered a double blow, for just when they most urgently needed
money, they found themselves laid off until the factory could be
brought back into production. (Unemployment of 12,000-15,000
was feared in Manchester because of the destruction of mill
chimneys.[104]) Many were left virtually destitute. In Balbriggan the
victims were:

for the most part cotton weavers, having their looms in their own houses,
and thus the visitation which has deprived them of their homes, has
deprived them also of their means of employment and support.[105]

On Killenarden Hill near Tallaght:

The weavers had fared worse. Not a house of them was left standing.
The Looms had broke loose and, like a man driving piles, had scattered

every standing wall. You would have thought it was the work of the Crowbar brigade. The weavers never said a word. Just quiet groups of them standing looking at what was left of their houses. They left the country without speaking to a soul. Where they came from we never knew, nor why. Where they went we never heard. God be good to them.

Spiralling labour and material prices made repairs impossibly expensive:

Straw is 18s. per load, and not a sufficient quantity to be had, even at that price, to repair one tenth of the injury.[106]

However, thatchers, slaters, carpenters, glaziers, nurserymen and masons had never had it so good. In Limerick slaters were asking a prodigious 7/6 per day, and in Drogheda they would not work for under 10/-.[107] People were up to all sorts of tricks. In Belfast, a man from the Falls:

went to Milltown cemetery and found out headstones which had been blown down. Then he wrote to America to the relatives of the people concerned. I understood that he made quite a good thing out of it.[108]

In Carlow one enterprising citizen:

on Monday morning, sold ten shillings worth of slates, which he had gathered in the streets, as blown from houses during the night.[109]

It was an object lesson in the workings of the market economy.

Who picked up the tab for the vast repair bill? Not the insurance companies. Though over twenty insurance companies were active in Ireland in the mid 1830s, most property was uninsured, the idea of insurance then being fairly novel outside the cities (where the different insurance companies had their own fire-fighters), the worlds of shipping and commerce and the wealthy elite.[110] Attitudes in the country may perhaps be gauged from an article in the *Tuam Herald*, which, for the entertainment of its readers, published a skittish article on how certain Scottish farmers had begun to insure their cows. Heaven forbid that such eccentric behaviour should ever spread to Ireland.[111] The lack of coverage, plus the fact that modern types of storm insurance were not then available, was one of the main reasons why the storm was such a disaster. This was good news for the big English insurance companies which then held most of the Irish market. The storm left them relatively unscathed. It was bad news for almost everybody else, especially the poor Irish tenant farmer who ended up shouldering the main burden of repair.

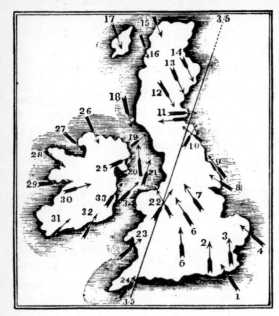

People attempted to piece together what had happened. This map showing wind directions between 10 o'clock and midnight on the night of the storm was produced by an American climatologist, James Espy. Do not let Espy's medieval looking map put you off, his orientations are accurate, however the winds were to vary as the night went on.

Given the storm's ferocity, the death toll was surprisingly low. Perhaps 250-300 people lost their lives. There were many lucky escapes. In Longford, an old thatched house two stories high was tumbled into the street, and though there were eight or ten people inside it at the time, by some miracle no-one was hurt.[112] Lord Castlemaine was less fortunate: he was struck by a gust as he closed a window and 'instantly expired'.[113]

The people of Cork seem to have led charmed lives: one man was hauling himself across St. Patrick's Bridge when the stone he had been hugging gave way, 'four or five tons of solid mason work' collapsing into the river behind him. Elsewhere in the city:

A young lady... alarmed by the violence of the storm, got up and went down the stairs to her sister. On her way down the chimney fell, carrying part of the roof with it, and forcing through the floor all the posts of the bed she had just quitted.[114]

In Galway at least seven died:

with a number of others in every direction of the town dangerously maimed

38

and bruised, many of whom will have to undergo amputation... It was heart rending to witness the number of interments which took place on Tuesday, and the piercing cries of their sorrowful friends.[115]

Most of those who died were lost at sea. There were several disastrous wrecks, the *Andrew Nugent* sinking with all hands off Burtonport, and the revenue cruiser *Diligence* going down somewhere off the Giant's Causeway, the 'entire crew' being lost. At least two dozen (and probably many more) vessels came to grief in the Irish Sea, the principal amongst them being the sleek transatlantic liner the *Pennsylvania* which was wrecked, then looted off Liverpool, along with fellow packets the *St. Andrews* and the *Oxford*, and an emigrant ship the *Lockwoods* (also looted), fifty-two of whose passengers drowned, some of them Irish people *en route* to New York under the aegis of the City of Dublin Steam-packet Company.

The ordeal of those caught at sea that night hardly bears thinking about. Off Killybegs the raging sea smashed seven fishing boats to 'peg wood', throwing others into the fields. In *Oíche na Gaoithe Móire*, Michael Burke describes the Atlantic as 'gone mad and jumping... and entwined with the clouds'.[116] Clearly the first thing to do if you were at sea was to get off it. Two men fishing off County Galway are said to have half-sailed, half-flown ashore, landing safely.[117] But not everyone could, or dared to land. Near Killala, in County Mayo:

a boat with eight men out herring fishing was sunk and all lost; and to heighten the misfortune the same awful blast which buried these men in the deep, unroofed their houses and left their widows and children exposed.[118]

Killala's story is the coastal experience of the storm in a nutshell. On Sunday evening Killala had two vessels at anchor in the bay, both of them small coastal traders, the *Earl of Caithness*, deep laden with a cargo of salt, and the *Wellington*, full of barley and oats, and bound for Belfast. When the dawn broke on Monday the *Wellington* was on the rocks and the *Earl of Caithness* lay capsized, her salt inexorably resuming the sea, and her crew of five:

lashed to her, with ropes, and the sea breaking mountains high over them, without any exertion made to save them.[119]

Their position was perilous. But help was at hand. When the news

'... four brave fellows jumped into a boat, which was soon lost sight of amidst the foaming surf.'

reached Killala several villagers:

jumped into [a] boat which was soon lost sight of amidst foaming surf. However these brave fellows persevered and in less than half an hour reached the wreck... rescuing from a watery grave, five of their fellow creatures.[120]

By way of contrast, for it was not all high drama, the crew of the *Wellington* were able to walk off at low water, hopeful that their cargo might be saved.

The general picture is similarly mixed. At Waterford, 'the vessels... rode out their moorings gallantly'. In the port of Limerick, however, chaos prevailed as boats 'burst from their moorings... though made fast by double stay of cable and chain', and in a mad fit of headbanging, cut themselves to pieces against Sarsfield Bridge, some twenty-five vessels being injured.[121]

3. 'The vault of heaven their only roof'

I trust something may be done by the Government to alleviate the sufferings of the wretches who are left destitute[122]

The story of the relief effort reads like a dry run for the Famine. There was a massive, urgent need for aid. What did the administration do? Nothing. At first sight this might seem to reflect British indifference towards Ireland's sufferings. But it was not. (Liverpool and Manchester, which were equally smitten, received no help either.) The explanation ran deeper, and involved the whole idea of what government was about. In the 1830s governments throughout Europe were only just beginning to appreciate that they might have some responsibilities in the fields of relief and welfare. Non-intervention was the rule. In addition, the Poor Law (Ireland) had just been passed, and few districts had Poor Law Unions (their formation being resisted by rogue elements within the gentry, who were in no hurry to increase their outgoings). So, even if the government wished to intervene, the apparatus to do so hardly existed.

In most places it was down to self help and charity. Schools were opened, soup kitchens were set up, and straw was distributed for thatching. Poor Law meetings were held and subscription funds established. In Drogheda that first Wednesday:

the most respectable and influential meeting we have ever seen in this town was held in the Tholsel[123]

with the object of helping the poor of the district. £400 was quickly raised, the roll call of subscribers being headed by a Mr. St. John Smith, who very thoughtfully confined himself to making a small donation, lest he appear 'ostentatious'. Aid for Ireland came from as far afield as Brighton, where the citizens of the town, led by a group of conservative expatriates, contributed over £100, as:

The Irish poor had not that resident gentry among them that the English had to assist them under such an affliction.[124]

But what if *noblesse* did not *oblige?* On the one hand we have the example of the Earl of Clancarty swiftly pledging a hundred pounds towards the relief of Ballinasloe, which was lightly damaged.

Fifteen miles down the road, however:

In Loughrea — wretched Loughrea — the wealthy agent of the Lord of the Soil takes the Chair at a Charity Meeting, and sets a noble example to all present by subscribing the munificent sum of Five Pounds[125]

The humanitarian impulse clearly beat rather weakly in some of the country's great landlords. The press sought to maximise giving, sometimes being none too scrupulous about the tactics used: the *Dublin Evening Post*, for example, reminding its genteel readership that though typhus:

arises from destitution and want, its ravages are often spread to the mansions and high places [126]

The newspapers, and in particular the conservative press, made it clear that wealth carried with it obligations, and that it was now time for these to be met. The gentry found themselves on trial. At angry local meetings the performance of estates was scrutinised, and if necessary condemned. Around Galway:

There was property to the amount of £5,000 which never paid a farthing towards the support of the poor [127]

a state of affairs that was no longer considered tolerable. (The meeting invited in the Poor Law Commissioners: henceforth such property would be taxed.) Absenteeism also came under fire, but it is impossible to make any correlation between residency and the levels of aid offered by individual estates. It is also difficult to gauge the scale of the relief effort. (The work of the Churches is hardly mentioned in the press, yet they must have been major players.) Likewise it is difficult to assess its effectiveness, though this must have been extremely limited.

Relief was also about the nature of the contract between landlord and tenant. This required the tenant to make good storm damage. However this was no time for dry legalism. As the conservative press appreciated, enlightened self interest now required that landowners make some investment in relief. Indeed, if they played their cards right, the storm might be an opportunity for them to do themselves some good.

Occasionally politics got in the way of relief. This was the case in Drogheda, where the relief effort was marred by an unseemly row. Just prior to the storm Daniel O'Connell's fundraisers had

*Poor people ended up on the roads 'the vault
of heaven their only roof.'*

'wrung' £100 from the town's Catholic poor. When the subscription
fund was set up some of his opponents thought that this money
should be exhumed from the coffers of the 'hater of protestants'
and distributed amongst the needy. Needless to say the money was
not liberated, but overcoming their scruples, his opponents pitched
in anyway:

eschewing all political considerations — and in so doing they acted as
became Christians and Protestants[128]

Those landowners who did the decent thing were generously
rewarded. As the *Downpatrick Recorder* put it:

one of the most pleasing duties that devolves upon us as public journalists,
is to record the kindnesses of landlords[129]

and they did so with a vengeance. The Marquis of Coyningham's
decision to allow the poor to clear his estate of brushwood (as
much a service to himself as them) prompted the *Drogheda
Conservative Journal* to reflect that:

Times of general calamity sometimes are useful in producing that exhibition
of Christian feeling and nobility of soul that exalts the character into true
greatness[130]

Disraeli, who once rather unkindly remarked that when it came to royalty, flattery should be laid on with a trowel, would have had nothing to teach the editor of the *Drogheda Conservative Journal*. In Balbriggan, as well as being grateful, the poor had to put up with the ministrations of 'The ever to be revered Mrs. Hamilton', the proprietor's wife, a:

charitable and tender hearted lady [whose] chief delight and study is visiting the poor.[131]

But it is wrong to mock. While it is poor that it should have had to come to this, in the vast majority of places, which had no ever-to-be-revered Mrs. Hamilton, the distress went unattended.

In the crowded west the situation was critical. Food shortages, typhus and cholera were feared. The price of foodstuffs was high even before the storm (potatoes were described as being 'at a famine price' that January[132]). The storm decimated reserves, with the result that in Connemara, where provisions were already scarce, there were widely voiced fears of famine. The unease was not confined to the western seaboard. In Drogheda:

The late awful hurricane, added to the high price of provisions, has reduced the poor of our Town to the greatest distress — many a poor creature with a large and helpless family have not where to lay their heads, and "gaunt famine" has marked them for his prey.[133]

In Cobh a mob prevented the export of potatoes.[134] The partial failure of the potato crop later in the year exacerbated the problem further.[118]

In the west, serious social dislocation seemed possible. Galway city feared 'an influx of strange paupers'.[135] Many of those who had just about managed to keep a roof over their heads seemed certain to end up on the roads or in the Workhouse, assuming they could find one. The position of many small farmers was also insecure. Assuming they had enough to feed themselves, how were they to pay the rent when the oat crop had been scattered? How were the cattle to be fed through the winter when:

the hay and straw... which in other circumstances, would be used as fodder for cattle and to make manure, must now go to re-thatch their houses?[136]

The *Pilot* predicted the 'utter ruin' of the 'poorer amongst the

Many sheep, goats and cattle did not last the winter.

industrious classes' (small farmers),[137] and many had to resort to desperate measures. Around Derry cattle survived by eating pulped whin-shoots.[138] A natural disaster was the last thing these people needed, particularly in the south-west, where the countryside was riven with secret societies, and inter-class and factional outrages were a daily occurrence. Rural violence was an important part of the backdrop to the storm, and at least one editor felt that the 'tempest' might just be enough to push certain troubled areas over the brink:

These deplorable tidings give rise to forebodings of a startling description and we very sincerely trust that the future may prove them groundless.[139]

However, while it heightened many of the pre-existing stresses in the social order, it did not upset it, at least not sufficiently to require reform.   As a result, the experience, potentially very instructive, was not profited from, and Ireland marched unreconstructed towards the Famine.

4. The journey into legend

T he 'Big Wind' of 1839 was a landmark experience, a horror that was in its way comparable with the Famine, for what the Famine did to life it did to property.   More people were made homeless during the night of the Wind than were evicted between the years 1850-80.[140]   It also gave the country a new year zero, a new 'date from which all things were reckoned.' [141] Those who lived through it were in no doubt as to its significance:

The oldest person remembers nothing like it — history records nothing like it... While we live — while our children live — while the history of our country is read — the storm... will not be forgotten.[142]

The Wind was clearly an extraordinary event, but was it unprecedented, as was often claimed? Probably not, but we would have to go back to the fourteenth century or maybe before to meet its equal. Bad storms struck in 856 and in 988, when a 'great and marvellous' wind ate its way through the midlands, chewing up everything in its path.   Late medieval Ireland also had to put up with at least two great storms, the greater being the only other named storm in Irish history: St. Mary's Wind of January 15th 1362, a tempest so boisterous that:

> The stone walles, steeples, houses and trees
> Were blow doune in diverse farre countrees[143]

Since then, Ireland has experienced hundreds of storms,[144] some of them severe, some of them memorable for reasons other than themselves, such as that which prevented Tone from landing in 1796. However, only one or two (those of 1548 and 1903) seem to have been in the same league as the Big Wind of 1839, which rapidly became *the* Irish storm. Were any of the earlier storms greater?   It is impossible to say.   Most took place before meteorological records began, and so we are lucky to know that they happened at all, never mind giving them a climatic profile.

The English experience is also relevant. England has had two epic storms within the last three hundred years, the Great Storm of 1703, which was catalogued by Defoe, and reputedly took 8,000 lives; and that of 1987, the only comforting thing about which was that it had the full battery of meteorological wizardry directed towards it and still slipped by the weathermen. Fortunately, neither of these really touched Ireland, England and Ireland tending not to share storms.

The Big Wind of 1839, however, was an exception to this rule. It straddled both islands, doing great violence to parts of Scotland, the north-east and the English midlands, and the coast of Wales (where it tore down much of the Menai Bridge, one of the engineering marvels of the age). It then crossed the North Sea to Denmark, after which it dominated the eastern Baltic for some days before finally dissipating. It was what A.B.C. Whipple would have called a superstorm.[145]

Meteorologically, when the data is untangled, and the good measurements sorted from the bad, it can be described relatively simply. The storm was the result of a deep depression centred to the east of the Hebrides (with an estimated central pressure of 918mb at midnight on Sunday at 58°N 11°W — making it one of the deepest lows recorded so close to the British Isles.[146]) This did not wander up from the tropics, it is more likely to have formed in these latitudes, and then moved eastwards across the British Isles.

But what caused it? It is hard to say. We live at the bottom of a dense and turbulent sea of gasses which is perhaps ten miles deep and perpetually in motion, agitated by currents flowing at different speeds, temperatures and pressures. When these volatile masses mingle, storms occur. The storm of 1987, for example, is thought to have been caused by a deep Atlantic low interacting with a pocket of warmer European air in the middle reaches of the atmosphere. As the warm air was less dense it rose, causing the air around it to rush in to fill the 'vacuum', creating high winds; a model which can also be applied to the events of 1839. This interpretation was accepted by both meteorologists and the general public.

In 1839, however, there was no such consensus. There was no single, unquestioned way of seeing and explaining. As a result, the interpretation of the Wind was not left to climatologists. Indeed, very few people seem to have been content with the idea that the Wind was solely a climatic event. This did their experience a disservice. There had to be more to it than that. In parts of Kerry it was said to have been sent by priests to punish unbelievers.[147] Others suspected the fairies:

people would tell you that... the English fairies came and invaded Ireland and that the Irish fairies raised the big wind and blew them out of it.[148]

After all, the night of the 5th of January was the feast of St. Ceara, when the fairies held their revels through the length and breadth of Erin. In *The Elder Faiths of Ireland* Wood-Martin writes that:

their last great assembly was in the year 1839, when violent disputes arose... and the night following a large portion of the fairy host quitted the Green Isle, never to return. The hurricane they raised in their flight was long referred to by the peasantry as 'The Night of the Big Wind'.[149]

the timing and the whirlwinds (Irish fairies have no wings and fly by whipping up a whirlwind — the *Sidhe Chora*) no doubt being seen as compelling circumstantial evidence that the Good People had had some part in it. (Richard Rowley writes entertainingly of their exodus being witnessed in Mourne.[150]) Or was it all down to Beethoven? The late 1830s had seen the Belfast premieres of at least two Beethoven symphonies. Had these done something strange to the upper atmosphere?[151] And what about the Masons? They were bound to be in on it somewhere:

old people say also that this dreadful wind was caused by the Freemasons bringing up the Devil out of hell... and that they could not get him back[152]

The kind of scientific analysis we now use to explain the natural world would then have cut very little ice. In the countryside people held fast to their traditional beliefs. If a cow sickened it did not have a virus, it had had the evil eye put on it. If the blackberries had not been picked by November 1st. they could not be gathered for they would have been kissed by the Púca. (As I browsed the newspapers of the day looking for storm damage, I came on an account of a court case in which witnesses testified to seeing fairies; and an instance of body-divining using a hay wreath lit by 'a blessed candle', reported from Cork — chance glimpses of a vigorous but fugitive culture.) Religious, scientific and 'traditional' ways of

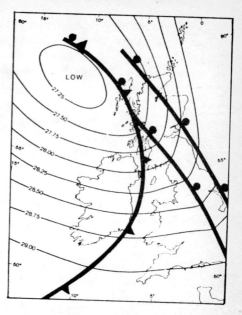

Proposed pressure pattern at midnight on the night of the 6/7th January 1839, showing the storm centre off the Hebrides. After Shields and Fitzgerald (Irish Geography, Vol 22, p40)

explaining the storm existed side by side, competing for people's hearts and minds, and it is hard to know which was the more widely accepted.[153]

The Wind was the last storm capable of inspiring this kind of philosophical confusion. The storm of 1903 was unable to cross the threshold into this rich land of magic, for the body of belief that might once have carried it there had by then been too badly eroded, with the result that it never became more than bad weather. This is what is poignant. The Wind of 1839 became a sort of gaelic *Gottedammerung*. For various reasons, most of them extraneous, it marked the beginning of the twilight of the era of mass belief in the old pre-christian gods. The more closely we look at the idea that the fairy host departed Ireland at the time of the Big Wind, the more symbolically true it becomes.

For most though, the storm was God given. The idea of the Wind as 'an awful visitation of his wrath'[154] permeates the reportage and the folklore; divine wrath being necessary to explain events of such moment. This is particularly true of the material contributed by subscribers and correspondents. For many the storm was a quasi-religious experience, and in some it induced a kind of religious ecstacy.[155] To many conventionally religious people (who also seem to have rejected the purely meteorological explanation), the Wind was sure proof that God lived. Some saw it as a privileged, cautionary insight into 'the dreadful day of wrath to come'.[156] As Malachi Horan who lived in the hills above Tallaght, County Dublin, put it:

Ay! God's wrath it was. Even the mountain men near died of the fright that was upon them. Like death the wind came to some, for the others it passed by. "Judgement, judgement, judgement!" it roared to every man.

Some, and this is perhaps more difficult to understand, saw it as evidence of His love for the world.[157] For a very brief period (a few days, maybe only a few hours) the country was brought to a very tender and very amenable spiritual condition.

This 'awakened state of feeling' led some Christians to examine and reflect on their faith, one by-product of which was a rash of poetry. All over the country people picked up their pens and started scrawling, the outcome being a crop of verse and religious musings, which appeared in the papers under innocent-looking titles like 'THOUGHTS SUGGESTED BY THE STORM'.[158]

Along the western seaboard, the storm also tapped a deep vein of millenial feeling, the most notable result of which was *Oíche na Gaoithe Móire, na Deireadh an Tsaoil* ,'The Night of the Big Wind, or the End of the World', a poem or chant of twenty-five verses composed by Michael Burke of Esker, near Galway, reputedly on the day after the storm.[159] Cast in the doom drenched tradition of Connemara religious poetry (the west was clearly ripe for evangelical missions!), *Oíche na Gaoithe Móire* compares the Big Wind to the biblical Flood, interpreting it as the *Ard ri*'s warning to the people of Ireland to change their lives, before it is too late.

Of all the verse written in the Wind's mellow afterglow, only Burke's poem has in any sense survived. That it stayed alive at all is not only a credit to Burke, it is a tribute to the vigour of the oral tradition. *Oíche na Gaoithe Móire* survived by being learnt, re-learnt and recited (a particularly fine recitation being recorded on Achill in 1957.) The journey into legend had begun.

That the storm was named also added greatly to its chances of survival. It isn't clear how it got its name but it is important that it did. At first it seems to have had many local names. In Donegal it was known as *The Night of the Andrew Nugent*, in County Tyrone it was *Montgomery's Wind* (pronounced 'Wine'), in parts of County Fermanagh it was *The*

The Japanese way. In Japan, sickles were placed at each end of the house at the beginning of the typhoon season, in order to cut the wind and save the house.

Night of the High Wind (also pronounced 'Wine'), and in Donaghadee *The January Gale*[160]). However, by the end of the century these various titles had largely become one: the Big Wind. Its namers were the plain people of Ireland, and this was its strength, for though it also captured the imagination of the middle classes, it was never catalogued in a way that was acceptable to them. No Defoe stepped forward to chronicle it. No significant literature appeared in English, and the Wind became the preserve of the poor, who made it their own, turning it into something enchanted.[161]

The storm generated a mass of lore. Stories by the million flooded into circulation. And when the Irish government's Schools Scheme sent 100,000 children off to dip into the folk consciousness in the 1930s, these were still there,[162] to be gathered by the children and transcribed in perfect copper-plate under *An droch-shaol* and *Cruadhtan* (the bad times/ hardship), where mention of the Wind is exceeded only (but decisively) by references to the Famine.

It is not surprising, then, that in *The Poor Mouth*, Flann O'Brien's glorious send-up of gaeldom and anglicisation (and everything else that was narking him at the time), when the hero meets his first *seanachie* the man 'fixed his backside carefully beneath him',[163] then told him a rescue story from the night of the Big Wind.

But the precious lore was dissipating:

It was ten years after the storm when my father was borned. His father told him the whole story of the storm but he has the most of it forgotten now.[164]

As time passed the lore passed with it, until in 1963 Kevin Danaher could observe that it had largely 'passed from memory'.

Why did it cast such a spell? The answer in a word is probably fear, plus of course people's helplessness in the face of it. For even though it was a greater communal experience than, say, the monster meetings of O'Connell, the storm was perhaps essentially a personal affair. It had its life in the hearts of the men and women who experienced it, and it is in the minutiae of personal experience, not the headlines, that we may seek to find its truth. Another element that made a deep impression was the sound of the wind, the unforgettable sound of the wind, often cited but never more than obliquely described. As Thomas Russell wrote:

The most terrible thing I have ever heard was the roaring of the wind on that awful night. I can never forget it, nor can any one who heard it forget it. I was too small a boy to go out with my elder brothers to assist in saving cattle and horses from tumbling down stables and outhouses, and every one of them was levelled — so, I don't know how the wind sounded outside; but in the house it was the most dreadful thing I ever heard, and it made the stoutest and bravest that heard it quail. The biggest battle that was ever fought since gunpowder and cannon came into use, might have been waged a hundred yards to the lee of the house and not a soul in it would have heard a single shot. This is no exaggeration. No one who did not hear the horrible sound — something between a howl and a roar — that the wind made on that night can form even a remote idea of its unutterable awfulness. It was hardly to be wondered at that almost every one thought the end of the world had come. Those who had probably never felt fear in all their previous lives were like babies, and wept like them.

The impact of all the above being doubled by the fact that the storm came during the night, climaxing in its deepest recesses, and that it came totally without warning. Then there was the profusion of weird wind effects, and the calamitous losses which were not only to be measured in pounds, shillings and pence, but in the personal tragedies of homelessness, amputation and lost lives.

It had other more subtle effects. Delayed effects. For as well as invading the folk-consciousness, it had insinuated itself into the annual cycle and its impact would only fully have registered when spring came — and nothing happened, or happened as it was supposed to, for what trees were there to bud and blossom, what birds were there to sing? So many things would have recalled it:

The storm's final metamorphosis was into entertainment, into tales of wonder and delight, that were told and re-told round the fireside.

the patched look of towns when people went in to market, the pasture rank with wheat and oats, and in particular, the strange mongrel crops that they would have harvested that autumn. Why did the Wind cast such a spell? How could it have failed to.

For the historian, this vast, but now much depleted folk memory is an invaluable way of making contact with the storm. The other great source is newspapers. In 1839 some 83 newspapers were being published in Ireland, seventeen of them in Dublin. There was a tory/protestant press (the titles of which included reassuring words like Conservative and Constitution), and a catholic/nationalist press (which published under titles such as Patriot and Liberator), and uncomfortably situated in the crevice between them a small clutch of liberal papers.

One reason the storm made so deep and so terrible an impression on those who lived through it was the extraordinary sound of the wind.

However, while Ireland was viewed from a range of political perspectives, it was covered from an elevated and relatively narrow social base. As newspapers were expensive and mostly available by subscription, their readership tended to be middle class,[165] and the further they stray from this constituency the less reliable they become. So the fact that 'the country' is always presented as being more seriously affected than the town may partly reflect the extent to which it was an unknown quantity to the townie journalist, and his susceptibility to the tall tales of farmers.[166] All the papers grieved over the condition of the country, but few took the trouble to send out a correspondent, depending instead on letters from subscribers, borrowed copy (there was no such thing as modern copyright law and the papers filched shamelessly from one another!), and lurid travellers tales.

The further one strayed from the printing office, the more mysterious the world became. To the cosmopolitan editor the people of the suburbs were shadowy figures, the rural poor an unknown race, sunk in superstition, visible as individuals only when they came in on Fair days or appeared before the courts. This is vividly reflected in the storm reporting, where the poor tend to appear *en masse* as 'poor creatures', their plight referred to in a general way; the language used to describe them being similar to that used for animals and livestock.[167]

Such foibles aside, the press rose well to the occasion. From Sunday night on, horrendous reports flooded into the newspaper offices. At first the damage seemed beyond computation, and the papers which published on Tuesday and Wednesday convey a sense of a society that was still reeling from the shock of it all, not least because many newspaper offices were themselves casualties, the premises of *The Pilot* being reduced to 'a ruin'. By the end of the week the tone is more sober, giving us two almost separate responses to the event, one from the heart, the other from the head, each accurate in its own way.[168]

Can the press be trusted? Did journalists ham it up? Undoubtedly. But not in a cynical spirit. If the prose was often as transcendental as the storm, it appears to have been so in an attempt to do it justice. (The inadequacy of words is a recurrent theme in the reporting.) The excesses appear to have been mostly of technique rather than observation, and the practice of reproducing copy verbatim, as opposed to re-writing it, worked strongly against exaggeration. Another factor to bear in mind before coming to any conclusion about the quality of the reporting is that much of what was published was written by people who lived in (and had to go on living in) the communities they were writing about. There were considerable forces working against excess.

T he return to normality took several months, and for some, who had lost loved ones or their livelihoods, there could be no going back to the way things were. By and large the storm had no important structural consequences. It had accelerated the implementation of the Poor Law, it influenced vernacular building: the practice of pegging thatch became more widespread,[169] houses were built 'in holes'[170] or sheltered places, with the gable (often a blind gable) facing west, so as to narrow the target area should the wind call again.[171] It was also thought to have led to the invention of the Robinson anemometer, by Thomas Romney Robinson, director of the Armagh Observatory, in 1843. The rest, including the in some ways central question of its psychological impact, is largely guesswork.

What trees were there to bud and blossom?
What birds were there to sing?

Materially, to an amazing extent, the country took the storm in its stride. The repair operation was massive, nationwide, but unnewsworthy, and it went largely unrecorded. For the viewer from the twentieth century, the silence is almost eerie. Within a fortnight the disaster had disappeared from the papers, its place being taken by lengthy accounts of matters such as the proceedings of the 39th meeting of the Commercial Travellers Society, speculations as to the *amours* of the nation's beautiful young queen, and advertisements for indispensable accessories such as Grimstone's Eye Snuff, 'a few cases of sight restored', and Incorrodible Parisian Dentures, that were it was claimed 'the toast of Europe'.

The memory of the storm was revived in 1909 when the introduction of the Pensions Act entitled everyone of seventy and over to a weekly 5/- pension. But who was over seventy? How did you tell when there were no written records? Enter the Big Wind once again, this time in the role of provider. If you could remember the Wind or put up a reasonable show of having been around at the time, you qualified for the 'pinshin'. (Tomás Laighléis recalled being sent to round up the old folk of the parish, ostensibly

The editor's world view tended to be rather — if there is such a word — town-centric.

to ask them about their memories of the Wind — a ruse to find out who was eligible.[172]) Of course, its amazing what you can remember if you've a good enough incentive. The last problem Asquith's government faced was one of benefit take-up — an estimated 128% of Ireland's pensionable population made a point of getting on the books (these old folk were no dozers!), a fact which caused much comment at Westminster.[173]

The Wind has by and large been ignored by historians, mainly, perhaps, because it is seen as an event that is all surface and no depth. It stands apart. It has no social origins, few social

Pension day. These old folk still had their wits about them!

consequences and it unseated no government. Its key failing, however, if one accepts that most history is propaganda of one form or another, is that it provided no-one with a political weapon (unlike the Famine, a weapon of nuclear proportions). No-one could use it to score points off their ethnic or class enemy.

Yet, as I hope the above shows, the storm was influential in areas which many historians do not recognise as legitimate areas of study, never mind have begun to investigate.

As for the storm, after bobbing to the surface in 1909, 1939 (the centenary, when there were splashes in all the papers), and lastly and almost imperceptibly in 1989 (for its 150th anniversary), it is again sinking without trace, settling itself amongst the Fir Bolg and the Tuatha de Danann in the mythological strata of the island. Where does that leave us, now veterans, by proxy, of the original Wind? Well waiting for Big Wind II of course (it isn't just Hollywood that loves a disaster!), the constituents of which, for all we know, may right now be massing off Rockall.

Storm
A—Z

Compiled primarily from newspaper accounts published
in the days and weeks after the storm.

Storm
A—Z

IRELAND has been the chief victim of the hurricane — *every* part of Ireland — *every* field, *every* town, *every* village in Ireland, have felt its dire effects, from Galway to Dublin — from the Giant's Causeway to the Island of Valencia.

It has been, we repeat it, the most awful, the most extraordinary calamity of the kind with which a people were ever afflicted.

The damage which it has done is almost beyond calculation. Several hundreds of thousands of trees have been levelled to the ground. More than half a century must elapse, before Ireland, in this regard, presents the appearance she did last Summer. The loss of farming stock, of all kinds, has been terrible. Many of the most thrifty and industrious husband-men, whose haggards and homesteads were filled with unthreshed corn on Sunday night, found themselves without a sheaf of grain in the morning. The poor, of course, as being the most numerous, have been the greatest sufferers. Tens of thousands of their wretched cabins have been swept away or unroofed — and many, as we have seen, have become a prey to the flames. On the whole, however, there has not been as great a loss of life as might have been anticipated. But the destitution to which they are reduced, must quicken the operation of the Poor Laws. In Cork, we perceive, that the citizens have already adopted active measures, with a view of immediately forming a Union in that city. A similar meeting has been held in Limerick — and we doubt not the example will be followed in other places.

We dare not call this hurricane a phenomenon, however rare or unprecedented its occurrence in so temperate a climate. But it will, nevertheless, become a study to our meteorologists. Trees, ten or twelve miles from the sea, were covered with salt brine — and in the very centre of the island, forty or fifty miles inland, such vegetable matter as it occurred to individuals to test, had universally a saline taste. The surges of the sea, therefore, must have been whipped up, and whirled hundreds of miles inland. Such, in a word, was the fury of the storm, that, had it lasted six hours longer, it is not houses that would have been prostrated, but streets and towns levelled with the dust. (D.E.P.)

If the Dublin Society was worth a straw — which for any practical and beneficial purposes it is not — they would before a month elapses, furnish to the public a complete and minute account of the mischief, done in every part of the island — of the effects produced in the course of the hurricane, on lakes and rivers, and of the law — if there be a law — as a late treatise maintains, which 'guides the whirlwind and directs the storm'. (D.E.P.)

The *Royal Dublin Society*, under an impression that an inquiry into the kinds and circumstances of the trees which have suffered during the recent storm might be productive of national advantage, by eliciting information as to the stability and strength of trees, and the adaptation of different types of soil and climate of Ireland, beg leave to invite communications on the subject, under any one or more of the following heads:

1) The number of Trees destroyed on any given space, with a description of the locality, nature of the soil, and elevation of the land, and the name of the place.
2) The kinds of the trees, and whether up-rooted or shattered, and the direction in which they have fallen.
3) The general size of the Trees, their probable age, and how computed.
4) Whether planted, raised from seed, grafted, or of natural growth.
5) General observations.

Communications, with real signatures, will be thankfully received by the Assistant Secretary. (notice in D.E.P.)

ANTRIM
(County) the accounts from Antrim are... deplorable (D.E.P.)

ARAN ISLANDS
County Galway
Sir, The storm here last night, which continued for eight hours unabated, was not only frightful but awful. The thatch and roofs of the greater number of the houses of the entire Islands were carried away, and more of them razed to the ground; some of the boats to the harbour are broken — some more swept away altogether; two or three cows and a horse belonging to Mr. O'Malley were killed... No lives, thank God, were lost... *your humble servant, Michael Gibbons*, P.P. (G.P.)

ARDEE
County Louth
The devastation... is almost incalculable... The Messrs.

Mulkittrick of this town are the greatest sufferers; a new stream mill of theirs which was nearly ready for grinding having been left a complete wreck, a very high chimney that was attached to it fell in the course of the night with a horrid crash, beating to the ground and prostrating everything in its course; such was the force of the storm that quoins of three hundred weight were absolutely blown out of the building and landed on the road a considerable distance from it... [One] might dwell long enough on individual suffering, and, yet fall short of conveying anything like the correct idea of the mass of misery into which so many persons have been plunged. Many a poor family are this night without a place where into reside; their houses are complete ruins... The surface of the river Dee was thickly covered with sheaves of corn, which had been blown from stackyards. (D.J.)

The sufferings of the occupants of the cabins is beyond description. Many persons have had to take shelter under hedges and in pig sties. One man's house together with a sow and a litter of young ones burned... Very fortunately he has a good landlord, W.P. Ruxton who of hearing of his destitution, sent him blanketing, and clothing. Revenue Police barracks and sixteen other good houses unroofed. A considerable portion of the beautiful steeple of Charlestown Church has been blown down, and at Ravendale and Claremount... upwards of £2,000 worth of timber has been prostrated. Smarmour and Thomastown have also suffered severely... no place has escaped. (D.J.)

The devastation in this town and neighbourhood beggars description. (D.C.J.)

ARDGLASS
County Down

The vessels in the harbour were completely wrecked. One laden with yarn, from Belfast to Drogheda, had her cargo saved; another was laden with herrings — it is expected they will be saved. The glebe house was so much injured that the Rev. Mr. Campbell was obliged to leave it... (D.R.)

ARMAGH
County Armagh

Has suffered very much. Many houses completely stripped and still more, partially. The gasworks are greatly injured; the chimney blown down, and the town in complete darkness. Great quantities of hay, corn, and flax blown away; in short... the country is nearly ruined. (B.C.)

ATHLONE
County Westmeath

The storm... has perhaps, in no other part of Ireland been more severely felt or more destructive to life and property than in this neighbourhood. It commenced almost instantaneously about eleven o'clock, and continued with unabated fury until half-past three in the morning. The town bears a most singular appearance, vast numbers of the houses having been totally unroofed... The artillery barracks and the large storehouses are generally damaged, the large ton slates having been torn off, and hardly a pane of glass remains. The two distilleries suffered severely to the extent of many hundred pounds; that of Mr. Robinson having a long range of coolers blown away, and otherwise sadly dismantled. The malt-house (Mr. Boswell's) was thrown down; houses of worship are in a very sorry plight; and the national school is in a fair way to promise an extension of the school holidays. A large range of cottages, at either extremity of the town took fire and... was totally consumed, and the unfortunate inmates had hardly time to save the clothes which cover them. The police, under Head Constable Smyth, acted in a most praiseworthy manner, and procured the barracks engine and a company of soldiers, which was the means of saving some of the houses...

It is a melancholy sight to see the poor people still hovering round the wreck of their former dwellings, trying to recover from the burnt pile something of their little property, and without means of subsistence, or a roof to cover them. The few cabins that braved the storm are crowded with the inmates of those destroyed — who, but for the charity of one or two gentlemen, would actually die from want.

The building which had been erected for a cholera hospital, latterly used as a corn store, was levelled to the ground, the roof and front walls having being blown into the canal, the back wall carrying beneath it a vast quantity of wheat and oats. The canal and Shannon have large masses of hay and corn floating about — the haggards of the unfortunate poor, along their banks, having been entirely swept away.

The gable end of a house at Esker... was blown down, killing a mother and three children. The house, shortly after, caught fire... the father, an aged man, and his only surviving child, were dug out of the ruins, dreadfully mangled and burnt, and are not expected to live. A poor man, in the suburbs... after his house had fallen in, was retreating with a young child in his arms, when he was blown into a bog drain and both perished. Vast quantities of trees have been torn up, blocking up the roads in every direction — the cross mails having to be forwarded by horse... (K.E.P.)

BALBRIGGAN
County Dublin
Few persons have passed through our town, latterly, without remarking upon its neat and improving condition, and we

had allowed ourselves to indulge in the hope that after the many vicissitudes and struggles to which Balbriggan had been exposed during the fluctuations and reverses of the cotton trade, it had at length arrived at a state of permanently increasing prosperity.

But it has been otherwise ordained — our town is now as though an enemy had sacked it. Fifty-four houses totally unroofed, and scarcely a single one of those that remain without considerable damage. The greatest exertions have been made, and are making, by the gentlemen of the town and neighbourhood for the unfortunate people... It is frightful to think of the condition and prospects of such a mass of our fellow creatures, should they have to remain without their houses... Mr. Hamilton is a heavy sufferer... his plantations a complete chaos. (W.C.)

More than two-thirds of the houses were unroofed — while many stood tenantless during that awful night — the unfortunate inmates, many in a state of nudity, banded together, had to resort to the streets. On the demesnes of Hampton and Ardgillen, upwards of 1,500 trees were like Gath's proud Goliath, laid prostrate — many of which withstood upwards of a century the angry scowl of proud Boreas. The magnificent mansion of Hampton suffered considerably... (D.C.J.)

BALLINASLOE
County Galway
Thirteen dwelling houses were burned to the ground besides several unroofed and tumbled down. (T.H.)
Garbally House... the seat of Earl Clancarty, suffered much damage; the finest trees were levelled. (G.P.)

BALLYGAWLEY
County Tyrone
Aughnacloy and Ballygawley, are little better than a heap of ruins. Some of the houses were blown down and others burnt. The inhabitants are in the most deplorable condition. Sir William Somerville's demesne has been completely sacked... (G.P.)

BALLYLONGFORD
County Kerry
The farmers in this vicinity have suffered severely... (D.J.)

BALLYMAHON
County Longford
...every house here has suffered — some levelled with the street, others completely unroofed — nothing but devastation on all sides. No lives have been lost, but the people are houseless and ruined. (T.F.P.)

BALLYMENA
County Antrim
The most extensive injury has been sustained here by the awful storm of Sunday night; houses unroofed and chimneys blown down, but no lives lost. The large

chimney of Messrs. Davidson's flax mills at Raceview has been blown down. It fell upon their gas works and demolished them. (U.T.)

Ballymena saw six people crushed to death when a factory chimney fell on them. (E.B.P.)

BALLYNAHINCH
County Down

The top of the new spire of the Church... fell through the roof, and carried all before it. The Roman Catholic chapel was dreadfully wrecked... Many thousands of the finest trees in Montalto demesne were uprooted or broken. Several corn stacks &c., blown away over the hills, and some of the farmers have suffered severely, both in their houses and stackyards. No lives lost. (D.R.)

BALLYSHANNON
County Donegal

The church is considerably injured; we believe it will not be repaired, and that Divine Service must be performed elsewhere until a new church be built. The Roman Catholic chapel on the Rock... the Methodist Preaching House on the Mall... and the roof of the Roman Catholic chapel, in the Back-street [are] much injured.

We have not heard of any lives (either of man or beast) being lost in the town. The country, however, was not so fortunate... several families [being] buried beneath the ruins of their dwellings. Along the sea coast the destruction of property is melancholy. (D.J.)

BANGOR
County Down

Holywood, Crawfordsburn, &c. — The plantations of Mr. Kennedy, Mr. Crawford and Lord Dufferin, have suffered most severely; many trees of noble dimensions, and thousands of young wood, have been blown completely out of root. Wind-mills, houses, &c., have all endured its terrible effects. (N.W.)

BELFAST
County Antrim

On Sunday night last and during the greater part of yesterday morning this town and its neighbourhood were visited by one of the most tremendous hurricanes that has ever occurred within the recollection of the oldest inhabitants. The beginning of the night was comparatively calm, a considerable fall of snow having taken place the day before, but about eleven o'clock, a violent westerly wind began to blow, which in the course of an hour or two increased into a complete tornado, sweeping everything before it... Chimneys were blown down — houses unroofed, walls laid prostrate, trees torn up by the roots, and consternation and alarm universally prevailed.

In many parts of the town the houses rocked as if shaken by an earthquake, to such an alarming degree as to compel the inmates to abandon them... In the morning the streets were covered, and in many instances entirely choked up with ruins, so as to be nearly impassable, and the scene of desolation which presented itself was truly frightful. (B.N.L.)

Wherever we turn our eyes, the most dreadful ravages of the hurricane are to be traced in our streets, squares, lanes, and unprotected suburbs, where — and especially in the latter — thousands have been bereft of a shelter. Such a scene of utter desolation we were never before called to witness. Houses erected but a few years — and some of them only a few months — left totally roofless; hundreds of upper stories rendered untenantable; and scarcely a roof, in the wide boundary of Belfast, unscathed by the unsparing tempest.

And, when the grey dawn of winter broke on the affrighted citizens, a scene of universal wreck and ruin met their eyes... We this morning found our streets without one exception, strewed with slates, tiles, and debris of chimneys, while, during the day, the shops were closed, as if a universal calamity had befallen the town. We repeat, that, within the memory of the oldest resident, such a storm has never been witnessed. Among the numerous accidents we have to detail are the following:

The chimney of Messrs. Mulholland & Co's flax-spinning factory, 184 feet high, has been almost wholly blown down, having destroyed a preparing-room in its fall, and a packing-loft was so seriously damaged, that it will be impossible to work in it for two weeks. The chimney thrown down at this manufactory was the most handsome specimen of masonry in the North of Ireland, and was supposed to be proof against the most violent elements. We are informed, that £1,000 will hardly cover the injury done at these extensive works.

The chimney of the Falls Flax Mill — a beautiful column, 150 feet in height, has also been blown down — and, a short distance up the same road, the chimney of Howie and Co's bleach-works was nearly levelled, though newly erected... We regret, also, to have to announce the fall of the splendid funnel shaft at Graymount bleach-green, near the Cave-hill... chimneys at Brookfield distillery... the Phoenix Foundry [and] the glass-house [were also] blown down... (N.W.)

The Barracks, we understand, have been severely damaged, and the Messrs. Lepper's extensive factory has also sustained serious injury. (B.N.L.) But the foregoing casualties were trifling [compared to] the loss of two lives, and other serious injury to life and limb, which this tempest has occasioned. By the fall of an old and exposed house on the old Lodge-road, a weaver... and his wife, were overwhelmed in the ruins; the former was killed, but... the latter was rescued, though in a very precarious state, in which she still remains. The large and beautiful new weaving factory of Messrs. Ledwich & Dickson, upwards of 150 feet in length, opposite the Lunatic Asylum, which had been roofed in a few days before, was prostrated to the ground, and the watchman killed. He was a quiet, industrious man — a Waterloo pensioner, and has left a widow and one daughter. (N.W.)

Some months ago... we called the attention of the mill-owners of Belfast... to the dangerous state of some of their chimneys, which, owing to the sinking of the foundation, had declined considerably from the perpendicular... Our fears have, unfortunately, been too soon realised... (B.N.L.)

The tower of the old White Linen Hall lost its lead covered cupola, which ended up near the gasworks. The Bank Buildings were completely unroofed, a large section of the roof landing in Arthur Square. In Donegall Street, a man named Fife, who was carrying a small child, was lifted off his feet and hurled against a wall, both were killed by the impact. (E.B.P.)
On the new Dublin road, the injury done by the storm has been particularly severe...

Wherever the streets or detached buildings were exposed to the gale, the damage done has been frightful. Serious injury has been inflicted on our merchants and shopkeepers, by the fall of chimneys, &c... Above 400 of the street lamps were damaged... (N.W.)
The brick wall at McClean's fields, a similar wall near the Covenanting Meeting-house, another at the head of Queen-street and a fourth in Donegall-street, have been levelled... in fact, there is scarcely a wall, of the description referred to, that has been left standing... about half past four o'clock yesterday morning a chimney in the rear of Mr. Robson's China Warehouse, in High-street, fell in with a tremendous crash, carrying with it two rooms in which were large quantities of gilt and plain China, fine Earthware, &c. all of which were totally destroyed... (B.N.L)

We understand that at Belvoir, the residence of Sir R. Bateson-Bates M.P. much damage... has been done, and even the castle itself has suffered. (Two stacks of chimneys fell into a room where two men-servants slept — U.T.) At Annadale, the oldest oaks were torn up by the roots... indeed there is scarcely a gentleman's seat, within many miles, respecting which we have not received similar disastrous intelligence... (B.N.L.)

In the rural districts... the tempest has been equally severe.

Haggards, stored with the rich spoils of harvest, have been scattered to the winds; and many a poor farmer, in addition to the loss of his livestock, by the fall of out-houses, will have to mourn the devastation of the grain crops on which he depends for the payment of his rent.

The farmers of Castlereagh, Moneyrea and Drumbo have suffered most severely. Trees, windmills, and houses, have been involved in indiscriminate wreck... (N.W.)

The *Ann*, of Belfast, is reported to have been totally lost on Sunday night, at Portpatrick, with all hands. The *Juno*, of Belfast, was lost on the same night, same place. The following casualties occurred in our Lough: the *Trial*, of Carlisle, laden with oats, and bound for Glasgow, ashore below Holywood — full of water, crew saved. The *Eliza*, of Killough, in ballast, ashore below Holywood — crew saved... Two sloops and one brig, ashore on Holywood bank. A sloop, said to be laden with barley, sunk in Garmoyle Roads; crew supposed to be lost. The ship *Glasgow* drove from her moorings in Garmoyle, and went ashore on the point of Holywood bank. A great number of vessels were also driven out to sea, the names of which we do not know... (B.N.L.)

BIRR
County Offaly
A great part of the barracks, as well as other houses blown down... In this neighbourhood, one boy and three females have been killed. (B.N.L.)

BLARNEY
County Cork
The drying lofts of the Paper Mills were blown down, and large quantities of the paper carried into the Blarney demesne, half a mile distant. (K.E.P.)

BORRISOKANE
County Tipperary
There never was such a storm as blew on Sunday night last... a few houses were thrown down by it, some were stripped entirely, and almost all more or less damaged; haggards of corn and hay were very much injured, parts of them driven quarter of a mile from where the stacks stood. A great number of trees were torn out of the earth; most providentially no lives were lost... (T.C.)

The chief part of Ormond brewery was blown down — four pinnacles were swept off the steeple of the church, together with a quantity of the tiles and slates — and the glebe house has been rendered uninhabitable. Two or three houses in the parish of Eggles have been consumed by fire... (D.J.)

BOYLE
County Roscommon
Boyle and neighbourhood came

in for its full share of the storm — upwards of thirty-six [houses] having been injured by it; the roofs of some of them altogether blown off. We particularly recognised those of the Misses Coyne, and the Misses McManus, in Bridge-street; all the out-offices of Mrs. Lloyd, on the Crescent; that of a man named Nicholson, on the Green; the roofs of which are entirely swept into the streets. (D.J.)

BRAY
County Wicklow
Roads at Bray, Loughlinstown, Kilruddy, Powerscourt, etc., impassable until a late hour of the day. A very fine young woman, living in a cottage opposite Mr Putland's lodge killed by the falling in of a chimney; her sister who was sleeping with her escaped with some bruises. (C.H.)

BRUFF
County Limerick
There was not one single house in Bruff that did not suffer more or less, some houses entirely blown down, others unroofed, and most of the town's people had to seek safety in the open street, lest their houses should fall upon them. Almost every person in the neighbourhood that had corn or hay in stack had this morning to look for it at a distance — some a mile or more. (K.E.P)
A family of the name of Mahony in Rathcannon had their house

burnt last night. The poor creatures, I am informed, had not time to save a single article, they lost, it is reported, £35 in cash, 7 firkins of butter, 8 feather beds, in fact everything they possessed, with hay, straw and oats. Some say it was malicious, others that it was caused by the high wind, which blew the sparks about. I am not sure which to credit. (K.E.P.)

BUNCRANA
County Donegal
The brig *William the Fourth*, of Tralee, laden with oats and bound for Liverpool, was forced from her anchorage in Swilly, and driven amongst the rocks off this town. The waves broke fearfully over the wreck — the hands on board were in a dying state. Early on Monday morning [four] intrepid volunteers succeeded in reaching the vessel, and had the satisfaction of rescuing seven human beings from their perilous situation. A dying sailor was immediately conveyed to the house of Rev. Hamilton Stewart, where he received every attention humanity could suggest and in course this good family had the happiness of seeing him eventually restored... Many other calamities have been occasioned by the storm — windows broken, haggards scattered, houses stripped and blown down. (K.E.P.)

BUNDORAN
County Donegal
At Bundoran the bathing lodges are nearly all blown down or unroofed. Several private residences have also severely suffered. (B.H.)

BURTONPORT
County Donegal
It is our painful duty to record the total wreck of the *Andrew Nugent*, the well-known trader... of Sligo: and it is still more melancholy to relate that Captain Crangle, whose body has been washed ashore, and every soul on board perished. The *Andrew Nugent* was wrecked at Rutland, on the coast of Donegal... In the morning she was found with her decks blown up, all the masts and rigging gone, and the shore strewed with the wreck. 992 casks of butter, and about 182 casks of provisions, in a damaged state, were saved. We are happy to learn that the owners... are fully insured... (T.C.)

CAHERGUILLAMORE
County Limerick
In Caherguillamore demesne, 200 cows were found dead having perished by the severity of the night. (L.C.)

CALEDON
County Tyrone
Two pinnacles were blown off the abutment of the steeple of the Caledon Church — one of them passed through the roof and gallery. (L.S.)

CAPPAGH
County Limerick
There were five vessels in the roads, and the *Hawk*, revenue cruiser, that rode out the gale in gallant style, while her consort, the *Hamilton*, was laid high and dry, alongside the Roadwall at Cappa. (L.C.)

CARLOW
County Carlow
The hurricane did serious injury in Carlow... though not, that we have learned, to the same extent as in other places. The Catholic Cathedral had one of the pinnacles of the steeple tower blown down... it will require some hundreds of pounds to repair the damage.
We heard of one man, who, on Monday morning, sold ten shillngs worth of slates, which he had gathered in the streets, as blown from houses during the night. The upper roofs of the most substantial edifices, and the walls down to their foundations shook, as if from the effects of an earthquake, and the great portion of the people of the town remained up all night...
In the outer parts of the town there was a greater number of cabins completely unroofed, and rendered uninhabitable...
A great number of the valuable trees on the demesne of Browne's Hill, on Mr. Faulkner's demesne at Castletown, and in other places, were torn up by the roots. Colonel Bruen's demesne wall was broken down in several

places. In short, so much damage was never heard of in Carlow... only the more terrific accounts from other parts of the country... afford the people reason to be thankful to Providence for their milder lot. (L.I.)

Mr. Thomas C. Butler... had a very narrow escape, having only left his bedroom when the ceiling was burst in by the weight of the chimneys. One of the back windows of the Club house, sash and all, were forced in, and shattered at atoms, and it required the united strength of the men to keep the shutters closed while means of security were being procured... (D.J.)

One of the ornamental spires that crowded the beautiful octagonal tower of the Roman Catholic Cathedral was blown off, and coming with great violence against the roof of the building, smashed it in, and came down on the front gallery, shattering it almost to a wreck.

The solitary chimney that topped one of the great towers of the ancient castle of Carlow, and which withstood the breeze for six hundred years, was also blown away... there has been great destruction of property, particularly on the Queen's county side, in the shape of corn in stack, cattle, trees, roofs of thatched houses, and hay, which have been scattered in all directions. (T.H.)

CARNMORE
County Donegal
Carnmore has become a scene of desolation and misery. (T.L.)

CARRA LAKE
County Mayo
At Carra Lake, and its vicinity, eight houses were blown down and destroyed, and the great, and ruinous devastation of hay, corn, and other agricultural produce, is to be deplored. (K.E.P.)

CARRICKFERGUS
County Antrim
The dreadful tempest was severely felt in Carrickfergus... houses, slated or thatched, were unroofed, even to the bare timber; corn and hay ricks, were prostrated... many trees were broken or torn up by the roots; and, in the Church-yard, a large sycamore tree, that had braved the boisterous blast of 140 Winters, was torn down, and, falling upon... two small cabins, exposed the terrified inhabitants to the "pelting of the pitiless storm." In many instances families were so much alarmed that they fled and sought shelter under some less exposed roof, and hence several families are now huddled into where only one was before. At day-light... though the tempest was somewhat abated, the tall chimney at Mr Barnett's distillery was seen rocking with each terrific blast. (N.W.)

CARRICK-ON-SHANNON
County Leitrim
At Carrick-on-Shannon several houses were blown down, others stripped of their roofs. The produce of the harvest lies scattered over the whole face of the surrounding country. (D.J.)

CARRICK-ON-SUIR
County Tipperary
...several houses fell, whilst many others were dismantled. One man, we have heard, was killed by the force of the storm... (W.C.)
In Carrick-on-Suir, Fethard, Urlingford, and indeed in all the towns adjoining, the hurricane raged with considerable fury... committing ravages to an extent quite unknown in this country. (C.H.)

CASHEL
County Tipperary
The damage done to houses here in Cashel, in the neighbouring towns, and along the country is very great; in some cases whole roofs have been carried off; cocks of straw, corn and hay were scattered about in every direction; in many cases inmates of houses were so alarmed that they were afraid to remain in bed. We are horrified to think of the dreadful disasters that must have occurred at sea. There was no fall of rain during the dreadful hurricane. (C.H.)
Several houses were completely levelled; the roof of a cabin fell in upon a widow and six orphans when in bed, and they narrowly escaped. The court-house, county infirmary, and palace, were much injured. Trees, which weathered the storm for many a year, have been levelled to the ground; an immense pear tree in Indiaville Garden, upwards of 100 years old, and fifteen feet in diameter, was torn up by the roots... The trees at Thomastown were blown across the road and a number of men were engaged the next day for a considerable time in clearing them away. (N.G.)

CASTLEBAR
County Mayo
Scarcely a person in the town remained in bed after the wind had increased to a storm; all were up, engaged in securing their dwellings, and prepared to make their own escape in the best manner they might. Very few houses in the town have not suffered in some measure...
Many narrow escapes occurred, from the falling roofs and from fire.
Mr. NEAL DAVIS was saved in a most providential way. He had been barricading a window in his house, opposite the church, and was about to quit the place when he heard a crashing noise; luckily he had the presence of mind to fix himself in the recess of the window, which he had scarcely done when the portion of the roof over his head fell in — passing so close to him that the timber or slates tore a part of his coat...
But it is to the houses of the poor

the greatest damage has been done — Five houses on Staball have been burned, and almost every thatched house there and in and about the town, stripped of the whole or part of the thatch or roof. That the entire of the houses on the street on which the fire broke out were not burned is owing to the praiseworthy exertions of the officers and men of the 87th depot, Mr. St.CLAIR O'MALLEY and the Police. As soon as the alarm was given the military turned out, and... risked their lives to arrest the progress of the flames...

The destruction of stately edifices, the property of the wealthy and the great has drawn forth many expressions of regret; but few could look without pity and compassion on the wrecks of the humble dwellings of the poor, thrown houseless upon the world... Mr. St.CLAIR O'MALLEY has done everything in his power to lighten and repair the calamity to these poor people; he has distributed money amongst them, and ordered them materials to reconstruct their houses. (M.C.)

CASTLEBELLINGHAM
County Louth
The beautiful demesne of Lady Bellingham has been destroyed. Upwards of 200 trees are prostrated. (D.J.)

CASTLECOOLE
County Fermanagh
Castlecoole has suffered severely, several thousand of trees have been uprooted. (I.R.)

CASTLE-FORBES
County Longford
Castle-Forbes, the seat of the noble family of Granard is now literally a scene of ruin — upwards of twenty thousand trees have been torn up... the offices have been unroofed, the green-houses blown to atoms, and the beauty of the demesne injured for ever. To attempt an accurate description of the ravages committed would be altogether idle, the fallen timber has rendered many of the walks impassable, so that months may elapse before the full extent of injury can be ascertained.

The tempest would appear to have selected this spot as the principal victim of its fury. In some places there are, as it were, furrows through the grove at least twenty yards in breadth and of incalculable length, where the stumps are still left firmly standing, about twelve feet high; just as if an immense park of artillery had discharged a vast quantity of chain shot into the very thickest of the woods.

The house itself, which formerly could not be seen except from the demesne, is now a conspicuous object from the public road. We cannot describe the feelings of pain and sorrow with which we gazed upon its ruined walls, and the desolation which surrounded it... It is a sad and affecting coincidence that during the very night in which his hereditary dwelling was suffering such losses, the body of the late venerable and lamented Earl was at sea on its way... to be consigned to the vault of his ancestors. Happy is he not to have lived to see the devastation of a place which he loved so well... (L.J.)

CASTLEPOLLARD
County Westmeath
Two houses were burned; many stripped of their roofs, and all more or less injured. No lives lost. (D.J.)

CAVAN
County Cavan
In the neighbourhood of Cavan, sixty three houses have been burnt. In one house alone, five pigs were found which had been literally roasted alive. Accounts from the sea-coast were truly frightful... (I.R.)

I cannot attempt to give you a description of the effects of the late tremendous storm here. Very little mischief, I am happy to say, has been done in the town of Cavan; but its neighbourhood presents a scene of devastation and ruin awful in the extreme. Throughout the whole of this neighbourhood the respectable farmer and the poor cottier have both suffered most severely... The demesnes of Castle Saunderson, Clover Hill, Drumkeen, Stradone, Ballyhaise, Lismore, Bingfield, and Kilmore, have all suffered irreparable losses; but the havoc committed by the ravages of the storm in Lord Farnham's demesne beggars description.

The noble woods of Farnham have sustained losses which neither time, nor taste, nor outlay can ever repair. In Derigid wood alone the loss is estimated at thousands, and here the majestic oaks, which had withstood the storms of two hundred years, have been torn up by the roots, or shivered as if by lightning, and have shared the same fate with the magnificent ash, beech, and elms. In one of the most thickly wooded parts of the deer park, almost every tree has been destroyed. I need scarcely say, that the beautiful gardens at Farnham have suffered dreadfully; over 1,500 panes of glass have been destroyed in the conservatories. The house has fared better than could have been expected; but the loss of thousands of the finest trees I ever saw is heart-rendering... (W.C.)

Lismore demesne wall, just completed, has been cut into sundry gaps, as every tree tore away all before it. The immense mass of timber prostrated cannot be removed for several days. Drumcarlan plantations (Mr. Bell's) are almost all laid prostrate, as are likewise those at Lismore. All the houses near the town are stript of slates... The grand sycamore at the gate of Castlecosby was uprooted, and thrown into the stable yard, carrying with it the gate and piers... The gaol and court-house are completely stripped... Ballinanaght town, through which I passed this day, is a heap of ruin, burnt to the ground, most awful and melancholy to behold — thirty families without a single roof to shelter them. (D.J.)

CLARA
County Offaly
We have suffered heavily in this town and neighbourhood. Some houses have been burned, others blown down, and the greater parts of them stripped. One of the concerns of the Miss Fullams has been reduced to a cinder, where there was nearly £2,000 worth of property, nothing worth mentioning has been saved... (B.N.L.)

CLIFDEN
County Galway
Seventeen bodies were thrown on shore near Clifden. (T.M.)

CLONAKILTY
County Cork
In the neighbourhood of Clonakilty the storm raged with great violence, houses were unroofed, and plantations ruined, and hay and corn blown about in every direction. (K.E.P)

CLONES
County Monaghan
A gentleman who left Clones at six o'clock yesterday morning, informs us that the storm committed great ravages in that town, Kingscourt, Cootehill, Nobber, Kilmainham wood, and all along the mail-coach road to Dublin. (G.W.A.)

CLONMEL
County Tipperary
We feel pain in stating that in Clonmel and its neighbourhood considerable injury was sustained. In the Main-street and Irishtown piles of chimnies were blown down — the roofs of houses partially carried away — and trees, which had stood the fury of the tempest for centuries, torn from their roots and scattered a considerable distance. (C.H.)
At intervals, during the night, heavy rain fell in torrents, which was blown so impetuously against the windows that several of them were dashed in and much damaged ensued. We have had some heavy falls of snow and hail since yesterday, succeeded by a partial frost. It is feared that the country districts have suffered much from the storm. (T.C.)

CLOUGH
Co. Down
A row of houses were unroofed. One man lost property to the amount of £200. Several of the inhabitants were obliged to leave their houses, and have not yet been able to return. All the grain in the vicinity has been scattered to the winds. Drumaroad chapel... has been completely levelled. (D.R.)

COBH
County Cork
Nearly every vessel in the harbour of Cove, drove, including her Majesty's brig *Rolla*, with two anchors down. The brig *Henry* and schooner *Eliza*, pilot cutters, *Mermaid* and *Seawitch*, were driven on shore, and several small craft sunk and stove. (C.C.) Many houses have suffered... it is most fortunate that we had the wind from the westward, otherwise the consequences would have been dreadful. (U.T.)

COLLON
County Louth
Its character, so unique, is gone forever. The magnificent wood of silver fir, which formed the western barrier, and gave such retirement to the temple and grounds, has been entirely swept away; nothing remains of it but a few broken stems, here and there, pointing out what once had been the pride of the late and illustrious Lord Oriel...
The American grounds, which have been so improved by his accomplished son, Lord Ferrard, are a scene of desolation; the towering pines, the rare black larch, the fine magnolias, the cedar, and Goa cedars, and other specimens of the rarest trees, which have been collected from all quarters of the globe, now lie prostrate — nothing can equal the desolation of the scene...
We hear the neighbouring seats have likewise severely suffered, but the proprietors appear to forget their own loss in that of this beautiful and perfect place, which all travellers and botanists have so justly admired. (W.C.)

COMBER
County Down
At Comber, the chimney of the Distillery belonging to Messrs. Johnston and Miller was entirely thrown down, and various other damage done. The other Distillery has also been injured, and the chimney of Mr Andrew's Flour Mill is levelled to the ground... (B.N.L.)
7,000 new bricks at 35/- per thousand were brought from Scotland to re-build the chimney of Andrew's Flour Mill. The top of Andrew's windmill blew onto the roof of the new Unitarian Church (then on the eve of being opened) causing such severe damage that the installation of a minister was held up for a year. (S.O.C.)

CONVOY
County Donegal
...suffered very badly. The hurricane committed serious devastation on the property of that excellent resident landlord Robert Montgomery.

COOKSTOWN
County Tyrone
...considerable damage has been done at Cookstown. I have just returned from visiting Red House, the demesne of W.P. Ruxton Esq., near this town and the appearance presented beggars

description... no progress can be made through the demesne without clambering over tree trunks. Mr Ruxton with the most humane feeling, has allowed the poor of the town into the demesne to carry off the brushwood for firing. (D.J.)

COOLANY
County Sligo
In the town of Coolany almost every house was unroofed; six or seven entirely felled to the ground. The house of a man named Commons was blown down at Carricknagat, and a fine young man named Andrew Commons buried in the ruins... Templehouse, the residence of Colonel Percival, M.P., is a complete wreck, scarcely a single tree left standing. Tanragoe, the seat of Stepney St. George, Esq., was greatly damaged. We are sorry to learn that sixteen excellent milch cows, the property of this gentleman, were killed by the falling of outhouses. (D.J.)

COONAGH
County Limerick
There are three dead... and a great loss of potatoes at Coonagh, by the inundation, whole pits being covered. (L.C.)

CORK
County Cork
We were visited on Sunday night with one of the most tremendous gales of wind ever remembered here. It commenced to blow hard at eight o'clock, from W.S.W., but at half past eleven the storm assumed a strength and fury almost irresistible, and continued with unabated violence until six o'clock on Monday morning, when it considerably lulled. Extensive damage, by the falling in of chimneys and unroofing of houses, has been experienced. The gable end of a house in Caroline-street gave way, and has caused much mischief to the houses adjoining.
Scores of chimneys fell — some through the roofs, and others into the streets. The largest and stoutest trees have been torn up by the roots; but that which best attests the uncontrollable force of the gale is to be found in the prostration of between 30 and 40 feet of the Balustrades of the western side of the Patrick's Bridge. The Dublin, via Cashel, Mail, was detained upwards of two hours by the storm. The guard (Connelly) presents the hurricane as the most furious he has ever remembered — the coach having been literally swept into the side dikes three or four times. The accounts from the coast are looked for with anxious solicitude. (C.R.)
Cork seems to have come off comparatively well. We have no loss of life, though in some instances the escapes have been singularly providential. In one, the family of a house had been warned of the dangerous condition of the chimney of a house adjoining, and the servant

maid had but time to quit her bedroom when it fell in through the roof. A minute later and she must have been killed. The roof of the house of a man named Daly on the Cork Quay, together with the back-wall, was blown in, and a large beam of timber, which supported the former, carried down through the floor. In its descent it struck the arm of a sofa, within about two inches of the head of a sick child that was lying on it, and went down through the next floor, leaving the sofa uninjured, and the child untouched. If, however, the city has escaped "comparatively" well, from all parts of the country the accounts are most distressing. The damage done, it is impossible to calculate. (C.C.)

CREEVE
County Monaghan
About fifty houses near Creevy have been destroyed by fire. The minarets were blown off our church, and my own habitation is almost a heap of ruin; the stables are totally destroyed. (B.N.L.)

CROSSGAR
County Down
Crossgar, and its immediate neighbourhood, have suffered considerably from the late storm. Universal alarm and consternation were excited. Many houses have been totally unroofed. Eight or nine families were compelled to abandon their dwellings and take shelter with their more fortunate neighbours.

Some of them, we fear, will not be able to return for some time. Trees, walls, and corn stacks have been prostrated in every direction. Lissara Meeting-house and Crossgar Catholic chapel have both been materially injured... (D.R.)

CROSSMOLINA
County Mayo
Almost every house in town was partially damaged. Four houses were consumed, together with a quantity of potatoes, &c, which they contained. The houses and plantations of the neighbouring gentlemen have suffered, but particularly Deel Castle, Rappa Castle, Carramore and Ballybrooney. But still more afflicting, eight persons were killed by the falling of their dwellings, and a man named Moore and his wife were blown away and drowned, whilst crossing a ford, in the parish of Kilfion. (M.C.)

DARNEY
County Donegal
...two houses entirely consumed by fire... one of them tenanted by a cottier of the name of McKey. It presented a melancholy picture to see his eight children running across the country to a friend's house, without a stitch of covering, their clothes having been destroyed by the fire. (T.L.)

DERRY
County Derry
On Sunday evening last this city

and its neighbourhood were visited by a storm of extraordinary violence... The two previous days a considerable quantity of snow had fallen at intervals, and throughout Sunday the air was keen and penetrating, but there was no indication whatever of the coming tempest. About midnight the storm broke out, the wind blowing south-easterly, from which point it gradually veered round to the south-west. It blew long and heavy gusts, between which the intervals were very brief, and brought with it rain which descended in deluges, and did not subside until about six o'clock in the morning.

So noisy was the elemental strife, that it must have banished sleep from every eye. In the morning there was not a street or lane in the city that did not exhibit proofs of its violence... The Court-house was much damaged, the glass in the windows of the Grand Jury Room having been shattered to pieces, and one of the scales in the hand of the figure of Justice in front of the building carried away.

We have heard of some providential escapes, owing to the roofs of the houses being sufficiently strong to support the stacks of chimneys which fell immediately above the beds where they lay. Mr. George Foster's rope-walk was blown into the river; but it would be vain to particularize the losses. In the neighbourhood a vast

number of stately trees were torn up, and some of the roads, particularly the one to Muff by Brook hall, were rendered impassable... For many miles around, in all directions, according to accounts we have received, the damage done has been very great, the thatch, and even the scraws of the houses of many poor people having been whirled into the air... (L.J.) Many of the huts of the peasantry have been unroofed or entirely prostrated, and in not a few cases... totally consumed by their thatch taking fire. (D.S.)

DERRYGONNELLY
County Fermanagh
...the Roman Catholic Chapel, which had been recently built at an immense sacrifice by the poor people of that district, has been levelled with the ground. (E.P.)

DINGLE
County Kerry
We have not been informed of any losses at Dingle, or its neighbourhood — except the destruction of few boats. (K.E.P.)

DONAGHADEE
County Down
Eleven vessels safe, eleven sunk or damaged. All the small boats afloat sunk and destroyed. Crews of all the vessels saved. Some progress has been made in saving the materials of the sunken vessels in Donaghadee harbour, which have been placed in the coast guard and harbour

work stores, etc. they lie in 15 feet of low water, and it is hoped that some, or all of them, will be got up. (B.N.L.)

The inmates of Captain Leslie's house had a very providential escape. One of his chimneys... not less than eight tons in weight, was precipitated through the roof, committing great devastation... (U.T.)

Steam packets between Portpatrick and Donaghadee have been disabled. (N.W.)

DONAGHMORE
County Down

Not only have thatched houses suffered, but in many instances slated houses lately completed, in the most permanent manner, have also suffered severely. The church here has suffered great damage — some of the stone pinnacles on its tower were broken off and precipitated through the roof. The damage done by overturning and scattering corn, flax, and hay-stacks, is very great. (D.J.)

In [this] parish... an immense stack of turf was, in an instant, lifted up about a foot from the ground and then dashed to pieces... (N.E.)

DONEGAL
County Donegal

In the town and neighbourhood of Donegal the storm was very destructive; we have heard of many severe losses sustained by the inhabitants. (B.H.)

DOWN
(County) .The county of Down has not been, as far as we can yet ascertain, an equal sufferer; but plantations were destroyed, and haggards, almost incalculable in number, scattered to the winds. (D.E.P.)

DOWNHILL
County Derry

The far-famed Mausoleum at Downhill House, county of Derry, was totally destroyed... (T.C.)

A poor hare, having taken shelter close by the pile, was struck and literally cut in two. (L.S.)

DOWNPATRICK
County Down

The storm exceeded in violence anything that can be remembered. It would baffle the skill of the most expert writer, to describe the feelings which must have entered every breast, when it was committing its ravages. The effects of the tempest are tremendous. Every paper teems with accounts of its fury in the different localities of the empire... All speak of an endless variety of unfortunate occurrences which it would be impossible to generalize.

The public buildings in this town have suffered much; the Cathedral, exposed as it is on an eminence, was greatly injured. In the grove adjacent to it, twenty trees were uprooted, the roof of the court-house was much damaged; seventy panes of glass were broken in the Infirmary, and the roof was materially injured; the damage sustained by private houses was immense; the inmates of many of the smaller houses, were running about in confusion, seeking security. Before proceeding to the detailed accounts, we cannot but notice a curious circumstance, which shows very strikingly the severity of the storm. In the country, about three miles off, a widgeon broke a pane of a window, and flew into a house seeking shelter, like the dove returning to the ark at the time of the general deluge...

At Finnebrogue... ash, beautiful elms, and aged oaks have been torn up by the roots. One in particular, which measured seventeen feet in circumference shared the fate of the rest. It is strange to remark that many of those which grew in a soft soil completely escaped, while others in harder ground fell beneath the blast... (D.R.)

The storms of 1796, 1803, 1821 and 1833 were little in mischief compared with this (A.D.D.)

DRAPERSTOWN
County Derry
On Monday morning the town presented a frightful aspect; desolation met the eye in every quarter. The ridges of three of the most splendid dwelling-houses in the New-street were entirely blown down. The elegant Market-house lately erected by the Worshipful Drapers' Company is partially injured, indeed there is not a house in the town altogether escaped unhurt. But the most lamentable scene of desolation is the parish church.

This... with its lofty steeple, in consequence of the romantic scenery of the surrounding neighbourhood, had a most picturesque appearance. Its aspect is now frightful; the spire is fallen and the walls are uncovered. The devastation was not confined to the buildings alone; many stacks of hay and oats were entirely blown away. Happily however, in the midst of such a catastrophe, so far as we know not one life has been lost (L.S.)

DROGHEDA
County Louth
Never within the memory of man has this town and neighbourhood been visited with such an awful storm... it subsided leaving this town a complete wreck. Few houses have escaped... Two or three cabins in the suburbs were burned, and many unfortunate creatures left houseless at this inclement season. The shipping in the river sustained no material injury, but we may expect the worst from those which were at sea... (D.J.)

The appearance of the whole town forcibly reminds one of a town taken by storm after a obstinate contest — the houses unroofed, many of them lying in heaps, the dwellers fled... trees in the graveyard uprooted. (D.C.J.)

Drogheda, as far as the town itself is concerned, escaped comparatively unscathed. That a great many families have been left without the shelter of a home, is unfortunately too true; but the subscriptions which have been so munificently and promptly recorded by the more affluent of our fellow-townsmen, will in a great degree alleviate, if not entirely remedy this evil. There have been many lucky escapes... Fair-street, Peter-street, West-street, and Shop-street suffered in a very trifling degree. The several breweries and distilleries are left unharmed. The large flax mills and manufactories, lately erected, have stood the brunt of the storm well... On the Quays very little damage has been done, if we except the carrying in of a great portion of the roof of Mr. M'Cann's house by the falling of a stack of chimneys. The Mayoralty House has been partially uncovered, as also the stores of the Messrs. Smith and Sons...
So much for the town; but we are sorry to add that the surrounding suburbs have fared badly, a great number of cabins being prostrated, and a still greater left totally unroofed. Those on the Northern and Navan roads have come off much worse than the southern suburbs. (thirty-two of the ninety or so houses in Windmill Lane had their roofs 'whipped clean away' — J.O.D.) Immense loss of property has been sustained in the immediate neighbourhood... We dread to contemplate the condition to which the agriculturalist must be reduced...
We very much fear that the price of food, which even before this calamitous occurrence was such as to cause serious apprehensions, will now be increased threefold... (D.J.)
Shipping: the brigs *Commerce*, *Johannes*, *Anna* and *Thomas & Nancy* were dismasted, with bulwarks and several timbers broken. The sloop *Endeavour*, of Drogheda, laden with coals, sank at Liverpool. Two drowned. (D.J.)

DROMARA
County Down
In Granshaw, near Dromara, a mother and her three daughters were killed with the house falling in. (D.R.)

DROMORE
County Down
This town though encircled by high hills has not escaped the influence of this dreadful tempest. Many houses are unroofed — many suffered more or less damage. During the night the poor people were well nigh frantic, imagining that some general calamity was about to happen, and there was some wiseacre, who gravely affirmed that — "It was no wind at all but an earthquake." (U.T.)
Many houses are unroofed — many more have suffered damage. The side wall of the

new Secession meeting house is blown down; and stacks of hay and grain have been scattered "to the four winds of heaven". (B.N.L.)

DRUMLISH
County Longford
...seven houses were burned, and thirteen thrown down; a young lad, about fifteen, lost his life. The chapel there has also been blown down. (L.J.)

A cabin was blown down, the thatch of which taking fire, ignited the whole, and, notwithstanding every effort to extinguish the flames, it was found impossible to check them, and no fewer than 36 dwellings and offices were entirely destroyed. (R.G.)

DRUMSNA
County Leitrim
About fifty houses blown down between this town and Elphin, immense destruction of property, especially amongst the plantations. (T.C.)

DUBLIN
County Dublin
The metropolis was, on Sunday night, visited by a hurricane such as the oldest inhabitants cannot remember — unbounded in its fury, and unlimited in its extent. Accounts are now pouring in on us, from all quarters, of its terrific and irreparable effects. Dublin, in many places, presents the appearance of "a sacked city." Houses burning, others unroofed, as if by storm of shot and shell, a few levelled with the ground, with all their furniture within, while the rattling of engines, cries of firemen, and labours of the military, provided the very aspect and mimicry of real war. (D.M.R.) The Dublin Society House [Leinster House]... the quondam ducal palace defied the storm. The trees in Leinster-lawn, of full growth, are scattered like prostrate giants on their mother earth. Sackville-street [O'Connell Street]... strewn with slates and brickbats... three houses suffered severely and a vast number of windows are broken. Fifty-one trees were blown down in Trinity College park. In Stephen's-green and Merrion Square few houses escaped the general desolation, stacks of chimneys being thrown down in every direction... the streets below being literally covered with slates and bricks. In Nassau-street, No 10, a glass-shop is a heap of ruins. In a calamitous fire in Mary Street six persons lost their lives. In Clare-street, a stack of chimnies fell in, and destroyed a female... The Churchwardens of St. John's humanely opened that church to shelter the numerous poor of the neighbourhood, who fled their tottering houses. In Sidney-avenue... a servant boy and a woman were, unfortunately, killed by the falling of a stack of chimneys.

In short, there is scarcely a street, nay, scarcely a house, which does not bear the impress of this dreadful calamity...

Irishtown Church... part of steeple blown down. The ball which surmounted the spire of St. Patrick's Cathedral was blown down, providentially without doing mischief... Simmons Court Church... steeple blown down. St. George's Church... most of roof off. Madame Stephen's Hospital... one wing roofless. Phibsborough Church... belfry greatly dilapidated, scarcely a house on the Phibsborough-road has escaped injury.

Rotunda gardens... largest trees blown down. Kilmainham Gaol... is the scene of devastation. Here the sentinel had a narrow escape... he had scarcely time to quit his sentry box before it was blown from its stand and scattered to atoms. Jameson's... malt kiln seriously injured, production stopped.

Considerable damage sustained on the banks of the Grand Canal, in the vicinity of Portobello and James'-street... the finest trees along the banks were blown down or torn up, and completely blocked up the road. Crowds of poor people were engaged during the day in carrying off the branches for firing... both on the banks and in the surrounding country, where the trees had in general been demolished.

In the suburbs and neighbouring villages the damage has been dreadful. In Rathfarnham the scene of devastation... baffles description. At Crumlin... Cromwell's Fort is totally destroyed... piano, glass, china, tables all making one common wreck. Kimmage Mills... chimney collapsed destroying mill. Rathmines... great devastation of ornamental timber all along the road.

Tallaght... chimney of the extensive paper manufactory blown across the road. Glasnevin... wall of Botanic Gardens crushed a sheltering policeman. Finglas, Castleknock... houses blown down, hay ricks carried away bodily. Shanganagh... stands firm as a rock, as does the column Sacred to Reform... one pane of glass was blown in, but through it the wind forced the shutters, and actually broke... a very strong iron window bar, fit for a prison.

Stillorgan... roads totally impassable. The same may be said of Donnybrook... in fact whichever way one turns, ruin and devastation are to be met with... The pleasures of those who remained out to enjoy the festivities of the Twelfth Night were dearly earned by their sufferings returning home. Amongst the most serious sufferers... was Mr Guinness, the eminent brewer. The back wall of [his] large stable was blown in... burying nine fine horses. The stall presented a pitiable spectacle — the noble animals stretched everywhere, as if sleeping, but with every bone crushed by the ponderous weight of the wall... (Abridged from D.E.P., D.M.R., D.E.M., T.A., U.T.)

The Bethesda Chapel was burned to the ground. At about half-past eight sparks were seen coming from the building, and the storm was so terrific at the time that what would be on another occasion deemed trivial soon spread into a most awful conflagration.

Nothing could exceed the awful sublimity of the scene. In a few moments the surrounding neighbourhood seemed in one vivid blaze of light, and coupling with this the howling of the tempest, the continued whirlwind of slates and broken glass, which were hurled through the air like so much sand — the cries of those who were obliged to abandon their dwellings, the ringing of bells, the rattling of creeks — all seemed to denote a city in a state of siege, the inhabitants of which had given themselves up to the most wretched despair.

About half-past ten o'clock, the Lord Mayor and the High Sheriffs arrived, where an order was instantly despatched to Island-bridge Barracks for a company of Artillery, with ordnance. These gallant fellows soon arrived, and commenced operations to prevent the fire communicating with the other buildings, but in vain. The engines, and the firemen from the different insurance companies made their appearance, but all their efforts proved useless, for in directing the tubes in order to extinguish the flames, such was the height to which the hurricane had arisen that the water was driven and scattered in the air, mixing in with the torrents of rain which poured down with unceasing violence.

It was then suggested that, in order to ensure the safety of the dwelling house attached to the church, the pieces of ordnance might be directed against the smoking ruins; but... the house had already caught the flames, and was shortly after enveloped in a cloud of fire.

Never was such a scene witnessed as at this moment. Every attempt was made to preserve the furniture from the destruction which threatened it, and a number of persons were employed to bring it out of the house; but such was the fury of the tempest, the chairs, tables, looking-glasses, everything, together with those who conveyed it, were driven along like so much chaff — so awful, so supernatural, in fact, was the strength of the boisterous element. About one o'clock, a house nearly facing the Bethesda, came down with a horrible crash, filling the air with planks, bricks, and dust of every description.

The circumstance of the devastating fire which destroyed the Bethesda, attracted crowds to the melancholy scene... the following day. (D.E.M.)

...the reckless daring of this distinguished corps was the theme of universal praise... nor were the new police deficient in the performance their arduous duties. (D.E.M.)

Three o'clock p.m.- We regret to say that a heavy snowstorm has just commenced, and that the wind is blowing almost as fiercely as it was at any period during the night. The worst consequences are to be apprehended should the gale continue, as there is scarcely a house the roof of which has not been injured...

Estimate of the damage done during the late hurricane, within the Dublin Police District, as reported by the Superintendents to the Commissioners of Police:

Amount of damage done

	£	s	d
Persons killed 2			
Persons injured 16			
Houses blown down 38	3,252	0	0
Houses partly blown down 119	3,949	0	0
Houses completely unroofed 243	4,753	0	0
Chimnies blown down 4846	27,190	0	0
Windows blown in 1527	4,520	0	0
Houses partially unroofed 1143	1,198	0	0
Panes of glass ascertained to be broken 30358	3,247	0	0
Valuable trees blown down 2534	4,659	0	0
Walls blown down 150	590	0	0
Miscellaneous damages not included in the above	10,687	0	0
	£64,045	0	0

The population of the district may be estimated at 25,000, and the number of houses at 23,000, which will give an average loss of five shillings to every inhabitant, and the... damage done to buildings may be estimated at a very low calculation, as £3 to every house. (G.P.)

DULEEK
County Meath
A bell, put up within the last week, on the summit of the Roman Catholic Chapel was dashed to the ground with a frightful crash. The steam-mill of Mr. Behan has been stripped of its slating and the roof of his dwelling-house adjacent to it similarly circumstanced. Balrath Mills about four miles from Duleek, took fire during the tempest, but the flames were extinguished... Agricultural property to an immense amount has been destroyed. (D.J.)
We are happy to state that the picturesque remains of the old Abbey at Duleek, adjoining the parish church, suffered no injury. (W.C.)

DUN LAOGHAIRE
County Dublin
Kingstown... escaped with... very trifling damage... a boat belonging to a fisherman named Daniel O'Connell sunk in the harbour. (D.E.P.)
The Liverpool mail, which left that port at five o'clock on Sunday afternoon, did not reach Kingstown until four o'clock this morning, having occupied thirty-five hours in the passage, which

was one of the most perilous on record. (D.E.M)

The effect of the storm was to render it totally impossible for any steamer or vessel to approach the coast and any [nearby] must have been driven out to sea... it remains yet to be told how they weathered the horrors of the night, or, if carried on the Welsh or English coast, what frightful tales of human suffering we have yet to hear. (I.R.)

DUNDALK
County Louth

Most of the houses and public buildings have been denuded of their roofs, and windows to a considerable extent destroyed. The Post Office in Earl-street has suffered very much, as between twelve and one o'clock the chimneys fell, tearing the roof and all the intermediate floors into the kitchen. The Barracks also suffered very much, and the new chimney at the Gas-house has measured its length on the ground. About 2,000 trees have been uprooted in the demesne of Lord Roden; several in the churchyard, in Bachelor's-walk, and on the ramparts, have shared a similar fate.

On the morning succeeding, the town looked literally as if taken by storm; the majority of the shops were closed; the lamp posts removed, the houses open to the sky, and bricks, timber, and slates scattered about in every direction. Stephenstown-house

and demesne, the property of M. Fortesque, Esq., have been injured to the amount of £500... (N.T.)

The postmaster and his clerk were waiting up for the arrival of the mail, when the chimney fell and carried them with the ruins into the cellar, from which they were extricated much injured. (G.W.A.)

The Postmaster and his Assistant were both so much injured... as to be unable to make up the mail-bags. (N.T.)

DUNDRUM
County Down

...suffered comparatively little. (D.R.)

DUNKINEELY
County Donegal

Since the year of 1803, nothing at all to equal the tremendous gale of Sunday night, or the extensive injury to property, has been at any time witnessed in this part of the country. This town, which is situate on an elevated site, suffered much from the effects of the storm. The house of James Crawford has been unroofed; the Post Office has been much shattered and the gable of the new corn store thrown down — every house has been... damaged. (L.)

DUNLEER
County Louth

The dwelling houses in this town were all injured... the losses of the poor farmers will be most serious... (D.C.J.)

Mr. Sherrard, agent to the estates of Rudolph De Salls, Esq., Sir R. Robinson, and Smith Barry, Esq., has received instructions from those gentlemen to examine what extent of damage the tenants on their estates have sustained by the late awful hurricane, and to render prompt and efficient relief to the sufferers, by roofing their cottages and otherwise indemnifying them for their losses. We have also been informed that Nicholas Markey Esq., of Walshestown, has humanely sent a large quantity of straw to be distributed among the poor of Dunleer, which village suffered severely by the sad calamity. (T.M.)

DUNMURRY
County Antrim
We have been informed that at Dunmurry very serious damage has been done to houses in the village, and also to the extensive establishment of the Messrs. Hunter. (B.N.L.)

EDGEWORTHSTOWN
County Longford
Sixteen houses unroofed, and all more or less injured. No fire or loss of life. (D.J.)

ENNIS
County Clare
The appearance of the town is dreadful — whole roofs thrown down — the slates torn off others, and the lead and tile blown off more. To enumerate the number of sufferers would be impossible... (D.J.)

Thirty houses prostrated, seven at Corofin, five at Quin. Four sailboats swamped at Bunratty. (T.H.)

ENNISKILLEN
County Fermanagh
The picture which this town presented in the morning was lamentable, the streets being strewed with slates, bricks, straw, and rubbish of different kinds. Hay stacks were blown down, windows in every house blown in or broken and many of the cabins in the lanes or back streets were blown down, but we have not heard of any of the inmates being killed or seriously injured. Among the buildings that suffered most we may reckon the Royal School at Portora... The barracks are next... The distillery has been nearly levelled, with the exception of the two tall chimneys, one of which lost only a few bricks — the other remaining quite perfect. The Roman Catholic Chapel in Darling-street suffered very much, the roof being greatly stripped, and the large stone cross on the front broken and blown into the adjoining yard. The greatest private loss we have learned was that of the proprietor of the White Hart Inn, Mr. Willis, who at a very great expense has recently rebuilt that establishment... his coach-houses, store and harness-rooms

were... entirely blown over and destroyed...

In Castle-Coole, the beautiful demesne of the Earl of Belmore, the number of trees prostrated is estimated at 15,000. At Ely Lodge, the Marquis of Ely's picturesque residence, the number is estimated at more than 2,000. At Florence-court... the damage is proportionably great, while the mansions in all have suffered. Crom Castle, that princely building recently erected by John Crichton, Esq. has suffered very much. Some of the castellated towers and chimneys are said to have been... dashed through the roof. (E.P.)

On Monday morning Enniskillen presented a frightful aspect; the shops were all closed as if death has visited the inmates of each; the streets were covered with broken slates, thatch, and rubbish.. An awful extent of damage has been done; windows broken and blown in; trees uprooted; roofs blown off; chimneys thrown down; floors forced in; cattle maimed and killed, and hay and corn blown away.

One man, who, living near the edge of the lake, went upon the roof of his house to preserve it by putting weights on it, and was himself blown away, and perished in the angry waters. It would be impossible for us to enumerate the losses sustained; but we may mention that... The large ballroom in the rere of Mr. Willis's Hotel, is in ruins, there is scarcely a pane of glass left in the front of the Townhall... One of the lightning conductors, bound to an immense strong bar of iron, in the Castle barrack, was beaten to the earth like a twig. The sentry boxes were upset in all directions... (I.R.)

A great part of the distillery of Messrs. Innis and Armstrong is levelled with the earth. The massive lead sheeting of the Gaol roof was rolled up and stripped off by the wind, like tissue paper. £2,000, we learn, will not repair the damage sustained by Portora...

The accounts from the country are most distressing. The poor people's houses are unroofed and some of them burned to the ground, hay and corn mostly blown away. Their prospects are most melancholy. May God pity and assist them under this most awful visitation of his Wrath. (I.R.)

FINNEA
County Westmeath
Finea and Kilgora have been burned. (D.J.)

FOATY
County Cork
At Foaty... not fewer than a thousand trees have been torn up. (K.E.P.)

GALWAY
(County) the scanty plantations of the county [are] half ruined. (D.E.P.)
The family of McCuskers, beyond

in the townland of Briarfield (trs.), were ready for it, and they knew the big storm was coming — because they had brought the devil up through the floor of their barn through their magic and got all from him. They had a servant boy hidden in a pile of wheat in the barn and he saw all the antics they were up to. The devil would not go without getting something from them. They asked what he wanted and he said he wanted a sheaf of wheat but they wouldn't give it to him for fear he would take the entire harvest the following year. So they gave him a cat and he had to be satisfied with it. (DIF MS)

GALWAY
County Galway
Never, probably in the memory of man has this town been thrown into such awful consternation as on Sunday night last, and had the storm been accompanied as on a former occasion with a spring tide... the inundation and destruction of at least half the town would have been the consequence. Seven lives have been lost, and there are four lying dangerously wounded.

From eleven o'clock at night to five in the morning the streets were impassable, as slates and stones were flying in all directions in rapid succession, chimneys falling, the roofs of houses giving way, windows smashing, men, women and children screaming and crying, seeking in vain, in many instances for a safe retreat, and some of them almost in a state of nudity. All were thunder struck and dismayed. The shipping was in a terrific & deplorable state. The vessels were at the mercy of the waves, no cable could withstand the shock... (G.W.A.)

Three boats left Galway on the morning of Sunday 6th instant, and were lost together with the following persons: [there follows a list of twenty-three names.] (G.W.A.)

The night of Sunday and morning of Monday last afforded an awful instance of the power of the Supreme... we will venture to say that the stoutest heart in our town was not entirely without alarm... as whirlwind after whirlwind succeeded each other with fearful violence, extinguishing the lamps and blowing down the old crumbling chimneys and ruinous roofs with which we are indeed overstocked in Galway. (G.P.)

The distress along the sea coast can hardly be imagined; poor creatures who have always indeed been accustomed to privation, have not now left even... a roof to guard their heads from the inclemency of a dreary winter, and many of them not even the walls of their cabins standing. Accounts from the country are if possible more appalling... (D.J.)

Let us, however, while this visitation is fresh upon the minds of the wealthy and comfortable impress upon them the necessity of rendering assistance to their fellow beings... How many has the Storm of Sunday night rendered houseless? How many has it rendered incapable of finding support, by the destruction of their boats or other little property. Alas! we might draw a dreadful picture, but the respectable house-holders of this town, do not need being forced into charity... (G.P.)

The meeting held yesterday at the Town Court House, for the purpose of calling on the government to send down one of the Poor Law Commissioners... was both timely and judicious... If something be not done previous to April or May next, the consequences we fear will be alarming. (G.P.)

GIANT'S CAUSEWAY
County Antrim
We feel it is our duty to announce the serious apprehension entertained of the loss of the *Diligence* Revenue Cruiser in the late storm, and her entire crew of forty-one men, besides some passengers. Her commander, Sir John Reid, was fortunately onshore, he having remained in Liverpool after his last cruise, and thus escaped a watery grave.

The *Diligence* was proceeding to the coast of the county Donegal. She came to, in Glenarm Bay, on the evening of Sunday of the 6th inst. and there took on board one of the Coast Guard, who had recently been promoted, with his wife and a family of young children, in order to land them at Donegal. It is supposed that the unfortunate cutter perished somewhere about the Causeway, as some oars, pieces of timber, and the stern of a boat, with the Queen's mark upon them, were washed on shore, near Ballycastle... (B.N.L.)

GORT
County Galway
Fifteen houses were consumed, besides an immense loss of property. (T.H.)

Loughcooter Castle, the splendid castellated mansion of Viscount Gort, was stripped of the coping stones, and many of the magnificent trees in the demesne prostrated... On the Gort road twenty-nine houses were burned. (G.P.)

GRANARD
County Longford
A number of houses have been levelled with the ground, not a stack of oats or hay have been left standing; and the largest trees have been uptorn in every direction. Seven houses have been burned; and several large turf-ricks in Kilgolgagh have also been consumed, where the houses of Mr. P. Woods, with all his valuable furniture, have been reduced to ashes. (B.N.L.)

The country people assert that they saw the fire falling down from the clouds, an apparent phenomenon, very explainable under the circumstances. It is estimated that in Granard several thousand pounds worth of property has been destroyed. (T.H.)

Granard escaped with some trifling loss. (D.J.)

GREYABBEY
County Down
This village comparatively safe; but the finest ash and elm trees in Rosemount demesne — some of them 4$\frac{1}{2}$ yards in circumference — have been uprooted. Many cottier's houses in the neighbourhood have blown down or unroofed; and hundreds had to seek shelter in the safer habitations of their neighbours. (N.W.)

HILLSBOROUGH
County Down
We have heard, from an eye witness, that Hillsborough has suffered very severely, both in trees and buildings. (U.T.)

HOLYWOOD
County Down
In Holywood the effects of the storm were quite as destructive as in Belfast, numerous houses being totally uncovered, and the inhabitants compelled to seek for shelter elsewhere; but the most melancholy occurrence is the death of... a man and a boy, who were found dead in a boat which had been drifted ashore near Cultra. The boy was found reclining on the man's bosom, to which, it is supposed, the latter had drawn him in the vain hope

of sheltering him from the blast and preserving his life, but both unfortunately perished. (B.N.L)

ISLAND MAGEE
County Antrim
A number of landholders have suffered very severely by the loss of stacks of... grain, blown down and scattered over the country, and, in various instances, wholly swept into the sea. Their houses are, with few exceptions, either partially or entirely unroofed, and the most distressing inconveniences and sufferings are now prevailing among many families there.

In Larne Lough... about five small coasting vessels, the property of sea-faring persons of that place, are run ashore... sunk and dismasted. Among the sufferers... are several small holders whose families [are] in a state of destitution and suffering. On their behalf alone the several Clergymen of Island Magee respectfully and anxiously supplicate the assistance of Christian friends... The smallest donation will be thankfully received at Mr. Phillips's, bookseller, Belfast... (N.W.)

JULIANSTOWN
County Meath
Ballygarth castle, the mansion of Colonel Pepper has been rent from top to bottom, and the glass dome, hitherto forming one of the most attractive ornaments of this splendid building, shattered to atoms. The loss of timber

here, as well as at Barmeath... is almost incalculable, in the latter place the monarchs of the forest, which for ages have bid defiance to the blast, are now fallen from their high estate. (D.J.)

KELLS
County Kerry

A great fire broke out in Kells, so as to destroy a great part of the town. (I.R.)

The fire broke out in a bakery, in which one man was burnt, being intoxicated... The exertions of the police were most heroic... the Chief Constable, Mr. Crawford... proving himself an efficient officer, and a feeling man. We deem it our duty ... to impress upon the government the necessity of appointing to such trusts men of energy, experience, and character, in preference to the "Bumpkins" who to a great amount disgrace this service... (U.T.)

KILBEGGAN
County Westmeath

Those who ventured out ran through their gardens into the fields, and hid themselves at the back of ditches. The gale continued with unabated fury for four hours and just at two o'clock the roof of a thatched house, on the Moate road, from which the inhabitants had fled, fell in and caught fire... In less than hour twelve houses, and everything in them were consumed, only an open space preventing the range opposite [plus a big distillery and adjoining corn stores] from going up in flames also.

What appeared to me to be the most astonishing effect of the storm was the blowing of the water out of the canal near this town. I visited it this morning and it was nearly dry. Slates from the Canal Company stores were carried 200 yards. A slate struck a large gate-post and nearly cut it across. This post was 157 yards from the building whence it had been blown by the wind. Those who saw it were lost in astonishment, and the people here have agreed to place it on top of a monument to be built on the spot to commemorate the horrors of the storm. (D.E.P)

KILCONNELL
County Galway

Mr Thomas Barrington, of Caramana, Kilconnell, impressed with a feeling for the misery produced by the late storm, urges that certain clauses of the poor relief bill should have practical application at once... so as to alleviate present misery and save vast future expense, through the avoidance of sickness and utter ruin to the poorer amongst the industrious classes. We certainly think that there would be the greatest prudence as well as mercy in the adoption of this course. (T.M.)

KILCOO
County Down

'And did the Good Folk ever come back to Dromena, Michael?'

'Deed an' they did not; an' a good thing too.'

'And why was it a good thing?' I asked.

'Sure they wouldn't recognise the place. A wheen o' years back a lot o' professors an' wild-like people come down from Belfast; an' they peeped here, an' they skellied there; an' they measured this, an' they dug that... an' they stuck up notices, an' pasted up placards, till if a Fairy happened on it today, he'd think he'd got into a museum by mistake. Aye', added Michael very bitterly, 'if ye were to watch in the Rath at midnight on May-eve, ye might find an' oul' professor wi' whiskers on him, but divil a yin o' the Wee People will ever be seen in Dromena again.' (T.O.M.)

KILGORY
County Clare
At Kilgory, whole plantations were swept away by the tempest, and the houses rendered almost uninhabitable, the lake, agitated in a frightful manner was driven into the drawing-room windows, destroying a valuable piano and other furniture. Mr. W. Molony, a visitor, alarmed for his domestic circle, endeavoured to reach home, was blown away from the road, and but for the shelter afforded by a cabin, must have perished... (L.C.)

KILKEE
County Clare
In the village of Kilkee thirty-two houses were unroofed, and a vast deal of damage has been done in the country to hay and straw, which are scattered in all directions. Several boats and canoes may be seen in fields at a distance from the shore. (B.N.L.)

KILKENNY
County Kilkenny
There were few of our fellow citizens who did not quit their beds in alarm, and several remained up during the whole night quivering about the hearth in terror as the house shook and the slates fell. Many quitted their houses fearful from the constant rocking... To increase the terrors of the night, about one o'clock the Tholsel Bell sent forth the peal of alarm — There are few sounds more dreadful to the inhabitants of a populous city, then the midnight alarm of fire. Hundreds were immediately running through the streets, seeking the spot where the fire was burning. There were fires at different extremities of the city, when three houses were entirely consumed, and their shivering inmates sent forth to seek shelter from their neighbours.
A sight awfully sublime, was presented at various parts of the night to those in whom the absence of terror left the liberty of contemplation. The moon shining but one moment with a sad light over the melancholy scene, and in the next becoming veiled by dark clouds that continued to chase each other across the sky — the crowds in

the streets, asking eagerly of each other where was the fire and scarcely waiting for an answer, while striving to avoid the showers of slates that fell about them — the rattling of window frames, the roaring of wind and water, for we could hear the latter — while the sparks whirled thickly along — served to render the scene one of terrific interest. It would be impossible to exaggerate, if we had leisure to describe it fully.

Early on Monday, we walked through the city, and everywhere evidence was given of the destructive power of the element... The windows of the barracks were *riddled*, and... many of the lateral architectural ornaments of the beautiful new Catholic Church of St. Canice, were broken off, though of solid stone work. [In] the Protestant Cathedral, the celebrated cross over the western window — the subject of so many wonderful legends — [is] broken off.

The gas chimney, at John's Green, upwards of one hundred feet high, and built but a few weeks, was tumbled down... damaging the works. Though elegantly, it was not firmly built. Many walls were also thrown down, and, in some gardens the walls fell, crushing valuable fruit trees. On the Upper and Lower Parade, on the Canal Walk... the destruction of trees has been very great.

In the town, however, though the damage is beyond amount, it is a almost trifling with the losses in the country. In the demesne of Jenkinson, the beautiful seat of Capt. Bryan M.P., upwards of 470 noble trees, torn up by the roots, were counted on Monday morning. In the garden, the sashes of the pine pits were swept over a wall of 12 feet high. The damage must, we fear, be greater than could be so soon ascertained.

The chief losses, however, have been sustained by farmers, whose haggards have been desolated by this dreadful visitation... Cabins have been swept off before the storm, and cattle have been killed... During the night men have ascended the roofs of their thatched cabins, and by stretching on them while the storm raged most high, sought to save the straw from being carried away. Rain has been everywhere... (K.J.)

KILLALA
County Mayo
At Killala, Westport, and we believe Ballina, the shipping was damaged; while the houses were subject to a similar fate... (D.J.)

KILLARNEY
County Kerry
In Killarney and its neighbourhood the hurricane raged with terrible fury. The town sustained much damage and many houses were shattered. Mr. James Goggin's chimnies were blown into the street, and caused that gentleman and the

whole neighbourhood much alarm — Mr. Michael McCarthy had a similar cause of terror, the roof of his house being laid quite bare. The windows of the Victoria Hotel were shattered to pieces and many aged trees... were laid prostrate, in every quarter and in all directions. (K.E.P.)

KILLOUGH
County Down
In the expressive language of some of the weather-beaten veterans of that ancient harbour, the land breeze, that as it were filled the streets with an irresistible flood of wind, was not a storm such as is usually experienced in the severest weather, but a species of hurricane sweeping across the face of heaven searching every corner and alley, and scattering abroad everything that was found weak in itself and without firm support.

No life has been lost here, but several houses have been unroofed, hovels blown to atoms, and the streets, in the morning, presented a confused mass of intermingled slates and thatch, on which were seen creeping a few isolated beings, driven out of their shelter at this inclement season. I am sorry to add that the pretty spire of the church, whose regular slating attracted the praise of every observer, yielded to the fury of the elements, and in its fall bent down the roof of the church,

leaving its vertex in the very reading-desk. (D.R.)

KILLYBEGS
County Donegal
The injury has not been so extensive as might be imagined; many places however, in and about, have been reduced to perfect ruins. The haggards — the poor man's hope and support — have been terribly damaged; corn stacks after being thrown down have been carried miles away in the breeze and forever ruined; many of them on the shore have been driven into the sea; hay stacks have been also thrown down and much injured. This destruction of the haggards, together with the loss of thatch all over the country, will have the effect of making scarce the fodder necessary for the cattle and of sending many to seek relief on the high-way or to the poor-house, which will immediately be required. In the harbour, on account of the good anchorage, the few schooners, the sloops and a wherry, have rode out the gale in good style. Several boats — I have heard of seven in the neighbourhood — belonging to fishermen, have been... smashed to pieces. Fears are entertained for the safety of the Arklow hookers and the wherries. (L.)

KILLYLEAGH
County Down
The chimney of Mr Martin's factory was blown down to

within twenty feet of the base...
and some of the property inside
damaged. The loss has been
estimated at £300. In the town,
the inmates of a number of small
thatched houses were obliged to
leave the next morning. One of
the small spires was blown off
the church, and many of the
slated houses were completely
unroofed... (D.R.)

KILMORE
County Down
Several families had to leave
their houses, and expose
themselves almost naked to the
"pelting of the pitiless storm".
Redemon Wood has suffered
much; one would think that the
woodman had set his mark on
every large fir, and laid it
prostrate... One of the pinnacles
lately erected on the church
tower was carried through the
roof.
A person of the name of Carvill,
who lives convenient to the
church, had his stable burned
down, and a fine mare much
injured with its fall... Lissara flax
mill is totally unroofed. (D.R.)

KILRUSH
County Clare
There are six vessels on shore
near Islevaroo, all of them more
or less injured. The *Undine*, the
Tar, the *Swan*, the *Providential*,
the *Dart* and the *George*. The
Undine has lost her keel, under
main boom, anchors and chains,
and sails blown to atoms.
The *Tar* has had her rigging

completely cut up — ropes, sails
and spars dangling in the wind.
The *Grecian*, a large vessel, that
was driven here in distress a
month ago, was torn from her
berth alongside the Custom-
house quay, and capsized in the
creek.
A boat laden with turf was blown
right under the arch of the bridge,
and is stuck fast there. The
Undine, of Limerick, was driven
on shore, and [four] perished...
(B.N.L.)
The loss of the *Undine* and the
death of Captain Robert
Patterson, his companion, and
crew, have occasioned a great
sensation here... most of the
shops in the town were closed
and every possible mark of
respect exhibited. The body of
Andrew Watson Mahony, Esq.,
was brought into town yesterday
morning (Monday) and two of the
seaman, named James Crockford
and William Cooper... a fine
interesting boy, of about 16. One
of the seamen saw Cooper
attempting to gain the rigging,
where the crew were, [but he]
was knocked down several times
by the sea... Mahony came by his
death from cold, fatigue and
exhaustion... the other two men
were drowned. (L.C.)

KINGSCOURT
County Cavan
The house looks as if it was after
standing a bombardment. The
injury to the country around is
incalculable — whole haggards
swept away and many poor

creatures... left totally desolate. The church is terribly shattered... no words can describe the awfulness of the majestic visitation. (D.C.J.)

KINNITTY
County Offaly
Much injury is done — and, I regret to say, that the roof of Captain Drought's house, of Lettyfield, has been blown in, burying Mrs. Elliot and another lady in the ruins. (D.J.)

KINSALE
County Cork
The destruction wrought in the Youghal and Kinsale direction, is not so considerable, as far as we can learn... (K.E.P.)

KIRCUBBIN
County Down
At Kirkcubbin, the brig *Henry Hastings*, laden with potatoes, is ashore with considerable damage; the tide ebbing and flowing in her.
Echlinville has been so much damaged that it has to undergo new roofing. Awful havoc has been committed in the surrounding grounds. One romantic old tree, which had reared its head for a hundred and fifty winters, whose branches extended thirty feet in each direction, fell a victim to the storm. (D.R.)

LANESBOROUGH
County Longford
As morning dawned the wind calmed down and what a sense of devastation they beheld! Roofs were blown out in the fields, sheep were dead by the ditches, woods had big gaps cut through them and hay and corn was everywhere.
The roof of Lanesborough chapel was carried off to where the new chapel is built, with not a straw out of place. People in Lanesborough are very fond of telling how God selected the site for their chapel. (DIF MS)

LAOIS
(County) suffered more than any county in Leinster. The destruction of trees is prodigious. (D.E.P.)

LETTERKENNY
County Donegal
Letterkenny Church, which has been recently rebuilt, was much injured, part of the spire having fallen upon the roof, and crushed all before it... The town generally, and also Ramelton, have shared in the casualties of this memorable storm. (L.S.)

LIFFORD
County Donegal
Suffered considerable damage, scarcely a house in it but was... injured. The roof of the church sustained much injury in consequence of one of the pinnacles falling upon it and forcing its way into the gallery. Trees were torn up here likewise — Mr George Knox, although his house in a great measure

escaped, suffered in this respect, having twelve apple trees, and two of another description, uprooted. (L.S.)

LIMAVADY
County Derry
About five o'clock the storm was at its height, and many persons were terrified for the consequences, and got up at that untimely hour. At day light the town presented the appearance of desolation — the streets were literally strewn with bricks, chimney pots and slates — the houses in many places completely stripped of their covering — the windows broken or dashed in. (B.N.L.)
Many of the houses suffered considerable damage... especially those situated towards the west of the town. (N.W.)

LIMERICK
County Limerick
At half-past eight the storm set in, blowing a rough gale from the West-north-west, which increased in fury every hour, until between eleven and twelve o'clock when it raged with all the horrors of a perfect hurricane, sweeping in violent gusts through the streets, and extinguishing all the gas lamps. The watchmen took refuge, in terror of their lives, under hall-door porticos, and archways, no living creature being able to stand in the streets, while the spirit of the tempest was careering in all his might through the air, streaks of lightning, at intervals, illuminating the midnight darkness, and a shower of slates at every angle which was exposed to the blast, strewing the ground with broken particles, and flying before the tempest, literally, we may add, like shreds of paper.
Not a public edifice or institution in the City escaped the ravages of the storm, all suffering material damage in the fierce encounter. The best built houses of the New Town... trembled in the rude embrace of their imperious visitor, and were sadly dismantled in the upper stories. House tops and flues fell prostrate, the crash of window glass was general and incessant, while, to crown the panic... a whole stack of chimneys would occasionally tumble down, after struggling with the blast like a drunken man...
The English and Irish towns, which constitute the abode of the less affluent and labouring classes, at every turn, manifest the devastating progress of the storm, by scenes of ruin and dilapidation...
A crowd of people gladly took refuge in the hall of the Exchange [where] they remained until daylight, many of them with only a blanket or sheet, for in their anxiety to escape... they never bethought of clothes.
Imagination will convey to the sympathising mind a better picture of the wild and dreary spectacle than description can

render... (L.C.)

The demesnes of Adare, Curragh, Castletown, Shannon Grove, Tervoe, Doonas, Hermitage, Tinerana, Kilballyowen and Ballinaguard, have suffered severely, many hundreds of the oldest and finest trees torn up by the roots. The chapels of Stone hall and Cappa, complete wrecks, not a vestige of a roof on either (D.J.)

The Club House roof was thrown down, Wellesley bridge greatly injured, owing to the vessels in the river being driven against it. The old Town suffered severely; some say there was over £36,000 worth of property destroyed... The mortality by the storm... for the port of Limerick, already comprises sixteen deaths. (D.J.)

There is a complete wreck of small boats in the river. Thirty sail boats left the quays on Sunday, after discharging turf and oats... We fear not half of them could survive... and already we have ascertained the loss of four down the river, three at Grass Island. A large sail boat, named the *Daniel O' Connell*, is also lost. John Hartigan, of the *Richmond Lass*, was killed... by a stroke of the jib-boom, which nearly severed his head from the body. At the Customs-house a capacious lighter, of forty tons burden, was thrown high and dry out of the water. (L.C.)

Sir, Amidst the awful devastations, any suggestion for future benefit is valuable. One

great cause of loss of life and property is the height and weight of the house chimneys, and for both of which... is Limerick conspicuous... if the tops of those damaged, and those to be built, were formed by short pipes of zinc, instead of heavy brickwork... [such] accidents could not occur. What is here recommended [is] in London... almost universal, *yours obediently, A Subscriber.* (L.C.)

LISBURN
County Antrim

On Sunday night last, this place was visited by one of the most awful hurricanes that has been felt perhaps for centuries. Trees that had stood the shock of ages now lie prostrate... and the roads in many places are completely stopped from the immense mass of trees lying across them. Some fine old trees in the Castle gardens, perhaps the largest in Ireland, [are] blown to pieces, one of them, known as the two sisters, has stood for centuries at the east end of the Centre Walk, has been smashed to atoms. These gardens present a melancholy spectacle today from what they appeared yesterday; and the surrounding country presents such a scene as baffles all description. The town too has received serious injury — houses stripped, and stacks of chimneys blown down in all directions. Several houses in the neighbourhood are thrown down, and the poor inmates left in the most deplorable situation. The damage done has been immense, and will require much time and expense to repair it. We look with much apprehension for the accounts from the country. (U.T.)

Obstruction of the Mail-coach Road: on Wednesday last we were asked to notice the neglect of the Very Rev. Dean Stannus as one of the Trustees of Turnpikes, in not having the trees removed from the road at Lisburn. In consequence of this neglect, all public and private conveyances on that immense thoroughfare by night and day had to turn out of the direct line, and pass through a narrow by-loning, to the danger of lives and property... (N.W.)

LISSADELL
County Sligo
...the seat of Robert Gore Booth, Bart., has been greatly damaged; thousands of trees, many of enormous size, have been prostrated in the demesne, several head of valuable cattle killed, and nearly all the outhouses reduced to ruins. Kevinport, the residence of George Dodwell, Esq., has been partially stripped, upwards of 100 tons of prime hay scattered through the country, and nearly all the young trees uprooted. Cooper-hill... presents a scene of desolation. The damage done is immense.
Ballytivan house was completely stripped, and a portion of the demesne wall thrown down. In this neighbourhood five houses

were gutted by fire, and two children perished in the flames. Two houses were burned in Ballinode. (D.J.)

LISTOWEL
County Kerry
The first house visited by the storm was that of Mr. McEniry — the roof was blown in and the inmates were only saved from instant death by the rafters, which formed themselves into an arch over Mr. McEniry's bed, where he and two children were sleeping... Several other houses have been materially injured, especially that well conducted establishment, the Listowel Arms Hotel. No lives have been lost. In the country around Listowel, the corn and hay have been scattered to the winds... Too much praise cannot be given to the Police who, under the direction of their efficient chief officer Chief-constable Fletcher, were conspicuous in rescuing from danger the inmates of those houses most exposed to the violence of the gales. In fact, through their unremitting exertions, many lives have been saved and much disaster prevented. (K.E.P.)
In and about Listowel the tempest, it appears raged with frightful violence... a full account of the ravages committed here would be impossible...
Ballybunion Castle, which for centuries had withstood the fury of the elements, is now a heap of ruins. (D.J.)

At Carra Lake... eight houses were blown down and destroyed. (T.H.)

LONGFORD
County Longford
Scarcely a house in the town has been exempted from its destructive effects, houses, both slated and thatched were stripped of their covering, and chimneys blown down in all directions... the quantity of glass broken exceeds count. The roof of the back of the new barrack... was as completely uprooted as if an explosion of gunpowder had taken place inside — the tun slates, laths, and roofing joist, which was 2½ by 4 inches, were carried off and strewed through the yard, broken in various directions, and the metal spouts which surrounded the building were blown away, and shared the same fate... (W.C.)
Not less than £1000 will repair the damages done the barrack alone. The church and Presbyterian meeting-house, and Methodist chapel have also been injured. The very neat and ornamented cottage near the artillery barrack, in which General Crawford and his son, the Rev. H. Crawford, one of our town Curates resided, has suffered most severely... Mrs. Crawford and her child... most providentially escaped only a few moments before a large chimney tumbled down through the roof which must have killed them had they remained...

Almost every house in Church-street [and] every house on the bridge has suffered; in fact, all those on the west side, particularly the one occupied lately by Kenny, the butcher, are so shook, that passengers are scarcely passing in front of them. Mr. Ganly's windows and sashes are completely shattered by the slates from the opposite houses; he also lost two fine heifers, which took shelter under a large hay rick, and which was blown down on them...
About twelve o'clock the canal burst in Farneyhoogan bog, about a mile from the town and rushed with great violence down the steep towards Killashee road, several poor creatures, who lived in bog houses, ran out with their families, up to the waist in water, hoping to save themselves. A poor man, named James Bracken, went out with his family; in a short time the force of the water and violence of the storm threw him down, with one of his children in his arms, and he never rose again; he was found dead on the side of the road in the morning; another of his children, and two orphans named Denniston, who resided in his house, were also lost... (L.J.)
They were brought in a cart to this town to have an inquest held on them, and a more heart-rending sight never was seen here... (T.F.P.)
The damage done to this town is estimated from £5,000 to £7,000, and the surrounding country has

the most awful appearance the human eye could perceive. (B.N.L.)

LOUGHGALL
County Armagh
Loughgall House and demesne have suffered considerably. A vast number of the splendid trees adjoining that beautiful house, the growth of at least two hundred years, have been torn up by the roots. The village and neighbourhood have equally suffered. (D.J.)

LOUGHREA
County Galway
One of the most destructive fires ever witnessed broke out in this town last night, about eleven o'clock. The fire raged with undiminished fury until six this morning destroying everything in its progress... Nearly 600 human beings were left destitute from this calamity, without a home, clothes or food. (C.H.)
It was utterly impossible to arrest the progress of the flames... Providentially the wind blew a little to the rere of the houses, and to this circumstance may be attributed the miraculous escape of many other buildings.
A meeting of the principal inhabitants was immediately convened at the Court-house, and subscriptions, for the relief of the unfortunate sufferers, were entered into on the spot. Robert D'Arcy, Esq., said he would communicate with Lady Clanricarde, (in the absence of

the Marquess) who, he was confident, would subscribe liberally. In the suburbs of the town, the damage done is incalculable. The ravages committed in the different plantations, haggards, farm-yards, &c., are most disastrous. (T.H.)
To relate the numerous instances of misery which have been related to us by an inhabitant of that now impoverished and desolate town would make humanity shudder. The wretched occupiers of those dwellings, with their wives and starving families, now call on all indiscriminately — for real charity knows no distinction — to assist them. (G.P.)
No town in Ireland suffered more than this once prosperous but of late years retrograding place... It was truly heart-rending to see the unhappy sufferers with their families, in the gloom of a winter's night, thrown on the world houseless and almost in a state of nakedness. Numbers would have perished except for the shelter afforded them by their poor neighbours, who, although themselves pent as to room, at once not only admitted them but, in many instances, quit their beds to make room for their more unfortunate street's-people.
The trees on the once beautiful Walk are swept away, and it is now a complete wreck. Many houses are unroofed in the main street; the Court-house is a riddle. Lady Clanricarde ordered the

fallen trees on the walk to be sold for the benefit of the sufferers; she also gave £20; Mrs. Daly, Mount-pleasant, £10; the Bishop (Dr. Coen), £5, and many others £5 each. The truly charitable Protestant rector, Mr. Medlicott, subscribed £6, and, with the Christian-like benevolence which he has at all times shewn towards the people of Loughrea, has sent £50 to Dublin to purchase blankets for the houseless hundreds, which are hourly expected...

It is but justice to state that but for the exertions of a few gentlemen — well seconded by [the] constabulary, it is difficult to say where the fire would have stopped. I am sorry to say there were wretches found, so far forgetting they were Christians, to indulge in robbing; several were arrested by Mr. Ireland, and the bacon stolen from the house of an industrious man found in their possession; it is to be hoped they will be made examples of. (G.W.A.)

LURGAN
County Armagh

Presents a most shattered array of houses ...with the suburbs and neighbourhood in desolation, impressing the mind with such sensations as one might feel in visiting a country ravaged by some ruthless enemy. The church has suffered severely, the spire thundered down with a fearful crash, burying the ball deep in the pavement, and injuring part of the roof. The spire of this church was destroyed by fire about 44 years ago. On that occasion the generous but ill-fated Munro happened to be in Lurgan, and though a Dissenter, and afterwards general of the rebels at Ballinahinch, he used astonishing exertions to save the sacred building; several times he so exposed himself, that the beholders turned their eyes away, expecting to see him topple from the giddy height amongst the burning ruins; and though the bell fell hissing from the belfry, this brave man continued his efforts till the fire was reduced and the church safe. What a pity that a character so chivalrous should ever have been seduced to join the ranks of sedition and combine with Popish rebels, who afterwards basely betrayed him because he would not consent to a midnight massacre. I trust I shall be forgive this short passing tribute to the memory of a brave, generous, but misguided enemy. In the Brownlow demesne about 300 trees were blown down... and in the Moira demesne, the property of the good Sir Robert Bateson, a vast number of trees have also fallen; amongst the rest, a beautiful row of elms, which in former time extended from Moira Castle to the village. (U.T.)

Church Hill, the seat of colonel Verner, had its roof completely blown off while thirty guests sat at dinner... (E.B.P.)

107

MAGHERAFELT
County Derry
We started about four [am]. The storm was terrible and the aged trees that lined the avenue waved fiercely as we passed along. More than once we were blown off the road into the ditch and had to hold on by the thorn bushes. When we came to the hollow of the road, before ascending Mullaghbuoy Hill, we found the road covered with water and impassable. To advance was out of the question and to return was the difficulty, for we had now to face the storm. We succeeded, although trees, standing when we passed at first, had been blown down in the interval and now lay across the way. The journey to town [Belfast] had therefore to be postponed till Tuesday; that day, as I passed along the top of the stage, it was dismal to see the dismantled houses, the broken chimneys, the fallen trees and the desolation produced everywhere by the tempest. (A.T.W.)

MALAHIDE
County Dublin
The cottages on the sea side of Malahide were rendered uninhabitable by the rise of the tide... (D.E.P.)

MALLOW
County Cork
Suffered much... Corn has, to a great extent, been blown about. (D.J.)
At Ballydanill, at this side of Mallow, a number of cabins have been blown down... On the demesne of Major Freeman, Castle Cor, and Sir Jephson Norreys, Mallow Castle, numberless trees have been uprooted and carried some distance from where they stood. The farmers are severe sufferers — scarcely a stack of corn or a rick of hay, we are informed, being left standing. (K.E.P.)

MARYBOROUGH
County Laois
An immense destruction of property took place in this town. (D.J.)
Fallon's Hotel was unroofed. The large dining room was left completely open to the sky. Mr Matthew Lalor's house fared little better. The end wall of Mr James Molloy's house on the corner of Church-lane, was split down to the foundation, and would probably have fallen to the ground had not massive planks been promptly applied as props... Smiths' forges, offices and buildings of every description were blown down or uncovered. In every part of the neighbourhood similar disasters occurred. (L.I.)

MOATE
County Westmeath
Imagination could not paint a scene more appalling than Moate presented — 63 houses were consumed. Mr. Robinson's haggard, containing a hundred tons of hay was burned. (D.J.)

Fifty houses are reported to have been burned in Moate, and two children killed. (L.I.)

MOBARNANE
County Tipperary
This road is completely shut up, and from the turn above the forge to the national school, is covered with large elm trees... The County Surveyor's men, who are repairing that road, very promptly posted up notices at the crossroads to prevent the carmen coming in contact with the trees, as no horse or carriage of any kind can pass until the timber is cleared off, which Mr. Jacob is getting done as quickly as possible, having a number of men with saws, hatchets, &c., clearing the road. (T.F.P.)

MOHILL
County Leitrim
At Mohill the dispensary and Roman Catholic chapel were a good deal injured. Mr. William Blake, of Farnaght, had a range of offices lately built, blown down, two heifers killed, and a corn mill completely unroofed. (D.J.)

MONAGHAN
County Monaghan
Monaghan has suffered — a dreadful fire has added to its horrors to those of the gale, and the town is nearly depopulated; a party of the 38th marched to protect the property of the unfortunate... (L.J.)
The inhabitants of the suburbs have... suffered severely, and many of the inhabitants of the town have suffered the same fate. (G.P.)
We are sorry to hear that Newbliss House, the residence of Dr. Kerr, suffered much from the effects of the late storm. Upwards of eight hundred of the largest trees were blown down in the demesne, and a splendid Church, building at the sole expense of Dr. Kerr, was much injured. (T.C.)

MOUNTMELLICK
County Laois
Seven cabins were blown down. Trees of immense size were torn up by the roots and carried away a long distance. (D.J.)

MULLAGHMORE
County Sligo
A number of fishing boats were smashed in pieces along the coast of Mulloghmore, and many houses carried away altogether. Scarcely a particle of hay or straw has been left in the country. Large hay ricks, containing from ten to fifteen tons, have been swept away, and are entirely lost to the owners... A report prevails here that the bodies of fourteen men have been washed ashore near Ballina. (S.J.)

MULLINGAR
County Westmeath
...suffered severely ...to the utter ruin of many of the inhabitants. (I.R.)
Those who had gone to bed were soon roused by their windows being blown in, or their roofs

stripped, and many persons who occupied old buildings, abandoned them altogether. Fortunately no lives were lost. Several small cabins in the outskirts of the town were burned, and almost all rendered uninhabitable. The Ward No.9 at the gaol was on fire for a considerable time, but through the exertions of Mr. Fielding the governor, and the turnkeys, it was put under.

The court-house was much damaged. The barracks, standing on an elevated situation, came in for the full fury of the blast... upwards of 1,300 panes of glass were broken. Murray's Hotel suffered severely. Mrs. Clark's hotel suffered even more than Murray's... In the country the damage if possible was still greater than in the town. (D.J.) To give an idea of the destruction done, would be to suppose the woods and plantations a corn field laid after a storm and rain, exhibiting here and there a few stalks standing...

Many houses both in the town and neighbourhood, have been levelled to the ground, some burned, and scarcely any escaped damage.

Hay and oats lie scattered in all directions... such a scene of devastation and misery was never seen in this part of the country as now presents itself to view. (T.H.)

At Streamstown, twelve miles off, the sails of the windmill turned so fast that the mill took fire. It

was badly burned. (Loc.Hist.)

NAAS
County Kildare
In this town the destruction is awful, hardly a house has escaped demolition. (C.H.)

'Mr. Doyle, you have often heard me spake of Murty Kavanagh?'
'Of Naas?'
'The same. He's gone.'
'Is it kilt you mean?'
'That's what I do mean, and so is his wife kilt, and his two children, and the house they lived in is gone and the town it stood in is gone.'
'The town of Naas is it you mean?'
'There is no town of Naas in it now. Every house in it is levelled to the ground.'
'Praises be to the Hand of God...' (T.B.W.)

NAVAN
County Meath
The whole face of the country is entirely changed. Scarcely a tree remains, and it will take a century before the damage done in a single night can be repaired. Arch-Hall, the seat of John P. Garnett, Esq., has suffered much. At Mountainstown, the seat of Arthur Pollock, Esq., not a large tree remains standing; the splendid plantations of Gibbs Town have been completely swept away. Headford, but it is useless to proceed; the vengeance of Providence appears to have been wreaked on this

miserable country and poor and peasant have all been the objects of its wrath. (D.J.)
The Lord Bishop of Meath has had 2,000 trees blown down in his demesne at Ard Braccan... (D.C.J.)

NENAGH
County Tipperary
Almost every family was up the greater part of the night, it being impossible to repose from the fearful howlings of the tempest. The Church, the Military barracks, and Fever Hospital have been denuded of their slates and tiles. The houses of the poor people in the suburban part of the town, above the old turnpike are all entirely stripped of their thatch and slates, the roofs in some instances blown off, and the walls burst out.
The roof of a house in Falvey's lane having been thrown in on the fire place, the thatch ignited, and the whole was destroyed by the fire. Were it not that the guard-house of the Military Barracks was humanely thrown open... many a human life would inevitably have been sacrificed. The houses in Castle-street, Silver-street, Barrack-street and Pound-street are dilapidated. (N.G.)
It would be an interminable task to enumerate the persons whose houses have been wrecked. One thousand pounds worth of trees, the property of Lord Dunally, on the Kilboy estate, have been destroyed... Part of the old Castle at Knight has been blown down. Three of the spires of the Church of Toomavara have been swept away — the Glebe-house, the Chapel, and many other houses in Toom, have also been damaged. (B.N.L.)

NEWCASTLE
Co. Down
Donard Lodge has been much injured. Several trees in the Park have been blown out of root. The beautiful appearance of the surrounding grounds has been much defaced. (D.R.)

NEWCASTLE
Co. Wicklow
Fever Hospital, Court-house, Bridewell, Barrack, Chapel, and number of private houses stripped of lead, slate and ridge tiles. A number of cabins in the town and neighbourhood levelled to the ground... The Chapel of Ashford has been totally unroofed... (T.H.)

NEWGROVE
County Clare
At Newgrove, the seat of Thomas Browne, Esq., over 3,000 trees were blown down, many of them have been the beauty and ornament of that fine demesne for more than one hundred years — the largest cedar in Ireland was amongst them... Kiltannon, Maryfort, Fort Anne and Tyredagh suffered severely... (L.C.)

NEWRY
County Down
On Sunday night, about eleven o'clock, the wind, which had been previously blowing hard from the north-east, rose suddenly to a pitch of fury rarely paralleled in this latitude, and, resembling the hurricane which so frequently spreads desolation and ruin among the West India Islands, continued increasing in violence during the whole night. There is hardly a single house in the town unstripped, and a number of cabins have been, we understand, completely wrecked. In the country, and along the shore, the effects of the storm are still more disastrous. Several ships, it is said, have been driven on land, more or less damaged; reports add that some dead bodies have floated in with the tide.
Lofty and venerable trees, which for probably a century defied the storm, have been torn up by the roots; the grain flax, and hay crops, stacked in haggards, have been overthrown and scattered; and the dwelling and office houses, particularly those with thatched roofs, much injured... The high wind which still continues will render abortive any attempt to secure the grain, &c. (N.T.)
On Monday... the streets were covered, in some places to the depth of more than a foot, with bricks, tiles, slates, mortar, and other materials of the injured and wrecked houses around. The damage done to houses and property throughout the country, is, we understand, extensive, and in many instances irretrievable... We have not heard of any lives being lost in our own town; but in the immediate vicinity, we believe, the inhabitants of the crazy cottages that are everywhere to be found, have not been so fortunate. (N.E.)
In the neighbourhood... a mother and child were buried in the ruins of their little cabin. (D.J.)

NEWTOWNARDS
County Down
...severely injured. Numbers of chimneys down and several houses stripped. (N.W.)
A small pig grazing at Scrabo was lifted and deposited in a tree some 400 yards away, from which place it [was] rescued by its owner. (E.B.P.)
In the wide district of Ards, scarcely a corn or flax mill has escaped, except Cunningburn mill, and Mr Bailie's, of Greyabbey, which braved the tempest unscathed. (N.W.)

OMAGH
County Tyrone
From this town we hear of some houses having been blown down, and others damaged by being stripped, and their windows shattered — the throwing down of stacks of oats and hay, and the... tearing up of trees, fill up the report of this calamitous visitation, which appears to have extended its ravages far and

wide, and to have spared neither rich nor poor.

The latter, however, who have been smitten by it, at the greatest sufferers, several families having lost their all in the destruction of their frail cabins, which have, in many instances, with all they contained, been consumed by fire. (L.S.)

ORANMORE
County Galway

Twenty houses in Oranmore are blown down or destroyed... the corn which the farmer had stacked for consumption or sale on the coming summer, now lies scattered over the road, or has been blown into the nearest river, a profitless waste, grief raising to look at when we consider what a dearth such a misfortune, being general, will surely cause the coming hard season. (D.J.)

OUGHTERARD
County Galway

...is, we hear, a scene of misery and woe. (D.J.)

PALLAS
County Galway

The house of an opulent farmer, named John Sullivan, at Pallace, near Killarney, was blown down, and having taken fire, was totally consumed together with a valuable haggard, three cows and twenty firkins of butter destroyed. He belongs to an industrious class, and sustained a loss which to him is irreparable. (K.E.P.)

PARSONSTOWN
County Westmeath

There is not a house here but has suffered much... several persons have been killed. At Riverstown, two young men were found dead in the ruins. (D.J.)

PHILIPSTOWN
County Offaly

The houses in Philipstown were dreadfully scattered. (L.I.)

PORTADOWN
County Armagh

The roar of the wind was like an uninterrupted cannonade, and every person in this neighbourhood thought that this terrible night would have been their last.

At length the morning dawned on a scene of devastation unparalleled in the annals of this part of the country. In fact, the losses which have been sustained in this neighbourhood, no money can repair, and will take two generations to make good. The scene, altogether is a heart-breaking one — but we ought to be thankful to Providence for the preservation of our lives. (I.R)

PORTAFERRY
County Down

Never was there such a tremendous hurricane witnessed in this place. I woke about ten minutes before one o'clock, when it was truly terrific. The appearance of the moon and the sky was indeed awful. We were afraid the house would have fallen. I have not lost more than 100 to 150 slates off the dwelling house. However, there is scarcely a house in the town but has suffered more or less. The blades of Mr. M'Cleery's wind-mill have been destroyed. The top of Mr Maxwell's mill at Ballyhenry was blown off, and killed four sheep that had taken shelter there. Six vessels were driven ashore in Ballyhenry Bay — only one rode out the gale. Two vessels at the quay became complete wrecks, and four others were considerably damaged. Many of the farms in the country have suffered severely... I have heard of stacks of wheat, both at Cloughey and Kearney, being carried into the sea. Some grain, supposed to be from Killinchy, came in at the shore at Bishop Mill, and I heard of sheaves of oats having been blown completely over the ferry from Kilclief to Bankmore shore... (J.U.A.H.S.)

Farm-yards have been bereaved of the hay and grain, which, in many instances, have been lost altogether. All the shipping in Ballyhenry and Ardglass roads, except three, drifted from their anchors, and were put ashore; and six vessels are still remaining ashore; in the former place, some of them considerably damaged, and will not be got off without being partially discharged. Three at the quay of Portaferry were also sent adrift by the violence of the tempest...

The beautiful demesne of Colonel Nugent has suffered much; one hundred and fifty splendid ash trees have been uprooted. (D.R.)

PORTARLINGTON
County Laois
No town in Ireland for its size suffered more than this. (D.J.)

PORTRUSH
County Antrim
...our infant harbour has well withstood the dreadful shock, the most tempestuous that ever visited the British Isles. Out of nine sail in our basin, only one schooner broke from her moorings, and went on shore... The vessel is somewhat damaged, but by the strenuous exertions of our active harbour-master, Mr. Delany, who is also an agent for Lloyd's, the cargo has been nearly all saved... (L.J.)

RANDALSTOWN
County Antrim
The town suffered little compared with the universal devastations elsewhere. But the farmers in the surrounding country are great losers, in consequence of their corn-stacks, hay, and houses in exposed situations, being in some cases partially, in others completely wrecked. (B.N.L.)

RAPHOE
County Donegal
In the demesne of the castle upwards of 130 of the most valuable trees were torn up by the roots, and sixty more so

broken that they must be cut down. At the former residence of the Dean of Raphoe, every third tree was blown down and in the demesne of William Fenwick, Esq., of Greenhill, similar effects are visible, in addition to which the declining house has suffered much, the lead having been completely torn from the roof... The roof of the Church is greatly damaged, and some of the trees which ornamented the burial ground are broken to pieces. (L.S.)
Palace at Raphoe — We learn that the Company with whom this beautiful structure is insured, have undertaken to rebuild it. (D.J.)

RATHFRILAND
County Down
Much damage done, but no lives lost. (D.R.)

RATHMULLAN
County Donegal
...at daylight this morning we observed that the schooner *Venus*... and the fishing wherry *Patrick*... had drove on the Inch Bank; the *Venus* had fallen over on her beamends, and sunk with her mastheads a few feet above the water, and the crew clinging to the rigging.
I am happy to say, (although blowing nearly a hurricane) the coast guard... succeeded in rescuing them. Part of the cargo (of whiskey, sugar, etc. — B.N.L.) may be saved. The wherry sank about four a.m., and the crew...

succeeded in reaching Fahan in their boat, with the exception of one man, who rashly attempted to swim on shore and was drowned... (L.S.)
Two puncheons of whiskey have floated ashore — they are taken charge of by the water guards. (B.N.L.)

ROSCOMMON
(County) These immense plains have been swept through with a Fury, prostrating everything in their course. The woods of Lord Lorton have suffered terribly and we regret to say that there have been many lives lost. (D.E.P.)

ROSCREA
County Tipperary
It is impossible to describe accurately the generality of the devastation; suffice it to say, that... this place presents to the eye of the beholder, one vast scene of desolation: and what added to the fury of the destructive element... is that there are entire streets out of lease those several years, and consequently in a dilapidated state, owing to this estate being mortgaged.
Several families have had hair breadth escapes: the house of Mr. Tinkler, Solicitor, had the roof entirely removed by one sudden gust... and the destruction of the cabins of the poor is indescribable... a young lad in the neighbourhood of Mount Heaton lost his life by a tree falling on him. (T.C.)

ROSS
County Wexford
Our private letters state that considerable damage has been done to the town of Ross — several houses shaken to the centre, chimneys blown down, and roofs carried away. We are sorry to state that the *Catherine*, of Newcastle, laden with timber... struck on the south tongue of our very dangerous bar on Tuesday morning. All the crew abandoned the vessel without delay, except the captain, mate and pilot, who courageously remained on board at all hazards. (T.H.)

ROSSCARBERY
County Cork
At Rosscarbery, a vessel that had been stranded, and was for some time lightening in order to her being got off was forced "high and dry" up on the strand and greatly damaged. (K.E.P.)

ROSSNOWLAGH
County Donegal
At Rossnowlagh and Coolmore there is scarcely a house habitable. The sea rose to such a height that the poor inhabitants thought it was the end of the world. Any grain or hay out was all destroyed.
The sand-banks, at the bar to our harbour, were so considerably lowered by the storm that in the vicinity of this town, a distance of about two miles, carts of sand could be gathered. The sea washed over the "Sugar loafs",

and boats could pass in a place where the tide had not before reached within half a mile. (D.J.)

ROUNDSTONE
County Galway
We learn that twelve men of the Roundstone coastguard, have been drowned, during the gale, the body of one only washed on shore during Monday. (L.C.)

SAINTFIELD
County Down
The entire top of the wind-mill of Mr. McBurney's was carried away; the iron shaft broken; and other damage done, to the amount of several hundreds of pounds. In Mr. Price's demesne, many of the most venerable trees were uprooted; and great devastation done to the plantations. In the neighbourhood, the rural population suffered to an immense extent. (N.W.)

SALTHILL
County Galway
There is scarcely a house in Salt-Hill that did not feel the awful effects of the storm, and it is inconceivable to think what ravages were committed. (D.J.)

SEAFORDE
County Down
Although Seaforde house has not suffered much injury, the demesne presents a melancholy spectacle. About 60,000 trees have been uprooted. The shrubbery bordering the lake,

with many other natural
ornaments, has been greatly
destroyed. The damage is
estimated at an immense
amount. (D.R.)

SKERRIES
County Dublin
Nine fishing boats with a crew of
from nine to ten men each were
lost on the Coast of Skerries.
(D.C.J.)

SKIBBEREEN
County Cork
In the neighbourhoods of
Skibbereen, Bandon, Clonakilty,
Bantry, &c., the storm raged with
great violence, and houses are
unroofed, and plantations ruined,
and hay and corn blown about in
every direction. (K.E.P)

SLANE
County Meath
I find it impossible to describe to
you the effects of the hurricane in
this quarter. As to the amount of
damage done, it is impossible to
form an estimate. (I.R.)
In this town the storm committed
great ravages... Almost all the
corn in the open air was blown
into the Boyne and over the
country. (D.C.J)
The Marquis of Conyngham's
demesne has suffered much; but
Beau Park... fared still worse. The
question is not now which tree is
blown down, but which is left
whole and standing. Every
avenue and walk is stopped, and
all the plantations are impassible.
The buildings... are so

surrounded by the fallen timber
that they cannot be approached
except by creeping under the
trees... that which on Sunday
night vied in beauty with any
place in the united empire is now
completely shorn of its
splendour. (D.J.)

SLIGO
County Sligo
To give a full description of the
devastation committed would be
morally impossible. Scarcely a
house in the town escaped
uninjured; chimneys, sidewalls
and roofs were shivered to atoms
- entire houses levelled to the
ground — shutters literally torn
from the windows of several
shops, and the iron bars twisted
as if by a giant's hand.
Nothing could exceed the alarm
created — the frightful screams
of poor, half famished creatures,
frantically flying from their
tottering homes, alternately
mingling with the roar of the
pitiless storm. Such was the
state of the town; but the country
has suffered far the greater
injury... several lives have also
been lost... (L.S.)
Hazlewood demesne, the pride of
this neighbourhood, has suffered
severely. It is worthy of remark
that many of the stately elms and
poplars on that ancient estate,
which have for ages defied the
fury of the tempest, have been
prostrated beneath the violence
of the late destructive hurricane.
Annaghmore, the seat of Major
O'Hara, has sustained great

injury, hundreds of trees having
been uprooted, and a number of
houses thrown down. Markee
Castle has suffered seriously.
Elsineur house, on the sea shore,
is irreparable... (D.J.)
On Sunday morning, six vessels
laden with grain left Sligo, and it
is feared they have all sunk...
(S.C.)

SPIDDAL
County Galway
The accounts from Spiddle and
other places along the bleak
coast are frightful yet we can
hardly found a hope on their
exaggeration. We are sorry to
hear that the Chapel of
Claregalway has lost its principal
aisle, and that one of the Gables
to the old Castle there has been
blown down. (G.P.)

STRABANE
County Tyrone
This town in addition to the
devastation committed by the
storm in the unroofing of houses
and blowing down of chimneys
was visited by an unusually deep
flood which rose to a
considerable height both over the
bridge and the lower part of the
Main-street, on the Lifford road
and up by the grain market,
owing to the heavy fall of snow
on the Saturday and Sunday
previous. (L.S.)
Strabane has suffered not only
from the storm but by the
inundations consequent on the
rain, which had so overflowed
the town as to prevent the Dublin
coach passing through. (D.J.)

STRANORLAR
County Donegal
The Meeting-house has been
much damaged — the roof
appears rent, and many of the
slates that covered it were carried
to a considerable distance. The
market-house of Ballybofey has
been unroofed, and is now
completely dilapidated... and
around that part of the country,
for miles, numerous proofs are
exhibited of the strength and fury
of the tempest. (L.S.)

SWINFORD
County Mayo
...several houses burned, and
many unroofed. Brabazon Park,
the seat of Sir William Brabazon,
received considerable injury, and
many of the largest trees in the
demesne were torn from the
ground. (D.J.)

TARBERT
County Kerry
The damage done to Tarbert and
vicinity is very considerable and
distressing: scarcely a home in
our village has escaped — slaters
and glaziers will have full
occupation for some time. Two
lofty heavy chimneys in my
house tumbled, partly on the
roof. We are indebted for the
preservation of our lives through
this awful night, to the
undeserved mercy of God. Of
course I remained up at night,
having secured my family as best
I could, in what seemed the

safest part of the house, for it was impossible to venture out to a neighbour's. No one could keep footing abroad or dare expose himself in the street — slates were flying about so thickly in all directions.

You may judge of the state of my mind, listening to the raging of the elements without, the crash of a tumbling house about me, and my fears excited, sometimes almost to madness... Our parish church is a sad sight... One of the heavy ill-judged pinnacles crushed in the roof, and destroyed the interior. The Roman Catholic chapel and National School-house likewise suffered.

In the country, stacks of corn and ricks of hay have been... scattered about like chaff... Several ships in the Roadstead, drew their anchors and seven or nine are now stranded on the Clare side... and it is feared all will be total wrecks.

Many an aching heart, and ruined family will the work of Sunday night leave among our people... There were large quantities of butter and lard &c., driven on Tarbert shore, which the inhabitants were getting, up to the hours of 5 o'clock, p.m. Monday evening. (K.E.P.)

In Tarbert every house has been stript, with the exception of Miss McMahon's hotel. The Police Barracks have been demolished; while the house of the Rev. R. Fitzgerald is totally dismantled... (D.J.)

TERMONFECKIN
County Louth
The losses here have been frightful. Newtown, the residence of A. McClintock Bird, Esq., has suffered severely. The old and venerable Demesne presents a truly heart-rending sight... The houses of the tenantry have likewise suffered much injury. It is much to be regretted that a good and resident landlord should have suffered so heavily, £2,000 will not cover the damage... (D.C.J.)

THURLES
County Tipperary
In the suburbs... many houses have been demolished; in the principal streets several have been unroofed, and glass to a large amount broken, particularly in our new splendid college... In this neighbourhood stood the interesting ruins of Killiney Castle, which for miles around was a very conspicuous land mark. It resisted the fury of many a by-gone gale, but, unable to withstand the hurricane of last night, it tottered, and now the majestic pile is levelled with the dust. (T.C.)

TRALEE
County Kerry
The disastrous ravages of the hurricane were awfully terrific and will long be remembered as exceeding in violence, the storm of 1814, or even that which dispersed the French Fleet in Bantry Bay forty years ago.

Much and serious damage has been sustained and the sufferings of the poor who live in damp shattered cabins, with very defective clothing, [are] greatly aggravated... there were many hair-breadth escapes. Mr. Richard Huggard, Solicitor, was just prepared to step into bed but delayed for a moment, to secure some windows from being forced in by the storm, when, in that short interval a stack of chimnies were blown down on the roof — smashing the bed to atoms, and carrying its fragments, with other broken furniture, through the floor to the drawing-room. The losses in agricultural produce were immense. It is feared that the loss of hay and corn will, in the ensuing spring, be very severely felt. (K.E.P.)
Mr. Splentz, of the Blennerhasset Arms Hotel, has been a sufferer to a very considerable extent in hay and corn — and Mr. McCarthy lost upwards of thirty tons of hay. An experienced person who viewed the country between the town and Ballyheige, on Monday, declares that £10,000 would not reimburse the owners for their losses in agricultural produce. A compact and well furnished brewery, the property of Mr. John Daly, took fire and was totally consumed. (L.S.)
...the poorer classes residing in the more retired lanes of this town have been severe sufferers; but we do trust that God... will inspire the hearts of the wealthy to play the "good samaritan" to them. (T.M.)

TRIM
County Meath
This morning the streets lanes and alleys presented one promiscuous mass of slates, tiles, bricks, stray, hay etc. Several houses have been completely blown down and the poor wretched inmates sent adrift to seek shelter... Church, Chapel, Grant Charter School, Military and Police Barracks and the Farm-yards, they present a truly pitiable spectacle — hay and corn lie scattered through the fields and along the hedges.
Slaters, glaziers, thatchers and labourers are in general requisition. The injury sustained must be immense.
You can form no idea of the distress of the poor people, and what an awful scene it was to witness at dead of night the shouts of men, the piercing cries of women and children... their lives in imminent danger from the flying of slates, bricks and other missiles. (D.J.)

TUAM
County Galway
Tuam has not shared the general calamity, its injuries being but trifling when compared with other towns. Although... a great many of the houses of the poor residing in the suburbs [were] thrown down [and] two cabins... burned. The Tholsel, or Market-house had the weathercock...

carried to a considerable distance out of town.

The residence of the Roman Catholic Archbishop and St. Jarlath's College — part of roofs stripped, with a great deal of glass broken in the latter. The Palace of the Protestant Archbishop — roof injured... many rare exotics destroyed. The Roman Catholic Cathedral — pinnacles thrown down, and the splendid Eastern window greatly injured... Our own Office — roof stripped, a good deal of glass broken. Part of the stables of the mail coach office knocked down — horse saved by the lofts which kept off the weight. (T.H.)

Our streets this morning presented a dreadful appearance. Instead of persons proceeding from home to attend their respective avocations, you might see groups at every corner, looking with consternation and surprise at the effects of the storm... (D.J.)

TULLA
County Clare
About nine o'clock this village was visited by a most dreadful gale which increased to a frightful storm during the night, scarcely a house escaped without the loss of roof or windows, many were completely blown down. The Church and new Court House were stripped, the lead of the latter twisted into the most extraordinary variety of forms, and blown far away into the fields.

The Glebe also suffered very severely, and had the demon of destruction excited the storm to devastate the country, his most ardent wishes were more than complied with. (L.C.)

TULLAMORE
County Offaly
The storm made dreadful havoc in this town and neighbourhood on Sunday night, it would be almost impossible to estimate the loss sustained in furniture and other property... two houses were burnt, a woman named Sherwin was killed in bed by the falling in of the wall, and a child... by the falling in of the roof. (L.I.)

The demesne of the Earl of Charleville suffered more perhaps, than any other place in Ireland. It is calculated that upwards of ten thousand pounds worth of timber has been destroyed. (K.E.P.)

The house of a poor sawyer, named Duinagan was blown down and he and his family were dug out of the ruins in a hopeless condition... To add to the misfortunes of the people of this town one of the great metal wheels that work the distillery of Messrs. Cuffe & Codd has been broken by the immense flow of water and that great concern which employed so many hands, will be left idle for some weeks. (D.E.P.)

TYRONE
(County) here the loss of agricultural produce has been

immense. (D.E.P.)

WARINGSTOWN
County Down
At the seat of Thomas Waring, Esq. a row of noble beeches were all prostrated. A melancholy accident is reported at Waringstown. After the storm had subsided, a tree... which had fallen across a wall bounding the highway, lay with its branches over the road; some persons were employed cutting off the top so as to remove the obstruction; a young man named Rowan had got upon the trunk; when the top was severed, the body of the tree, springing to its vertical position, struck Rowan on the breast, and flung him backwards over two corn stacks; he was taken up alive, but without hope of recovery.
One farmer in Aughanoon, had about thirty stacks of oats blown through the country, some of the sheaves being carried to about quarter of a mile distant.
Maralin Church received some damage... The distress of the poor at this inclement season will be lamentably increased, as there is not perhaps in the whole parish a thatched house undamaged. (B.N.L.)

WATERFORD
County Waterford
On Sunday night last, we were visited with the most terrific storm we ever remember to have experienced. There was but little rain, and no thunder, or lightening — nothing indeed but the wind blowing tremendously and furiously, and continuously from midnight till after five o'clock... The scene which presented itself on Monday morning, exceeds any we have ever witnessed in this locality... all presented an appearance of the utmost desolation. (W.M.)
Scarcely a house in the City escaped without damage; almost all the streets were covered with slates, tiles &c., blown off the different houses — but the storm seemed to vent its greatest fury on the upper part of the town. In the avenue leading to the House of Industry, three large poplar trees were torn away... On the Gallows-road two cabins were completely dismantled. On Morrison's-road two cabins were blown down, as was also another in Robert's-lane... the gable end of a house in Cannon-street facing the Artillery Barrack was also torn away. The leading of the National Bank Office was literally rolled off, as though by the hand.
Two families who resided in Goosehill... became alarmed at the violence of the storm, and fled affrighted from the house, the roof of which, they truly feared, was about to fall. Unfortunately, fire had been left in the grate in one of the rooms, upon which the thatch fell. The flames instantly communicated, and notwithstanding immediate alarm, and a numerous

attendance, that and an adjoining house were consumed, nothing having been saved, except some trifling articles of furniture, which were, however, broken by being thrown into the street. Thus several unfortunate creatures have been rendered homeless and destitute...

Bianconi's Kilkenny Day Car was delayed about an hour, in consequence of an obstruction by trees, which fell at Flood-Hall... (W.C.)

The vessels at our quay rode out their moorings gallantly. (W.M.)

WESTMEATH
(County) The loss of life and property in this county has been frightful. (D.E.P.)

WEXFORD
County Wexford
Owing to the low position of the town, and the consequent shelter it received from the high grounds to the westward, the action of the wind was not so terrible in its effects as it has been in other places less favoured by their natural position. The vessels in port, we are happy to add, all escaped uninjured. (W.I.)

There is scarcely a house in the town, in which some members of the family did not get out of their beds in the greatest terror. (W.C.)

The visitation fell on Wexford with peculiar fury. The town, however, being built in a hollow has escaped. (D.E.P)

WICKLOW
(County) Great devastation among the plantations of Lords Fitzwilliam, Rathdowne, Wicklow, and Powerscourt. (D.E.P.)

Abbreviations:
A.D.D.: A Downpatrick Diary; A.T.W.: Autobiography of Thomas Witherow; B.H.: Ballyshannon Herald; B.C.: Belfast Chronicle; B.N.L.: Belfast News Letter; C.H.: Clonmel Herald; C.C.: Cork Constitution; C.R.: Cork Reporter; D.S.: Derry Standard; D.R.: Downpatrick Recorder; D.C.J.: Drogheda Conservative Journal; DIF MS: Department of Irish Folklore Manuscript; D.J.: Drogheda Journal; D.E.M.: Dublin Evening Mail; D.E.P.: Dublin Evening Post; E.B.P.: East Belfast Post; E.P.: Erne Packet; G.P.: Galway Patriot; G.W.A.: Galway Weekly Advertiser; I.R.: Impartial Reporter; J.O.D.: Journal of Old Drogheda; J.U.A.H.S.: Journal of the Upper Ards Historical Society; K.E.P.: Kerry Evening Post; K.J.: Kilkenny Journal; K.M.: Kilkenny Moderator; L.I.: Leinster Independent; L.: The Liberator; L.C.: Limerick Chronicle; L.J.: Londonderry Journal; L.S.: Londonderry Sentinel; L.J.: Longford Journal; M.C.: Mayo Constitution; M.R.: Morning Register; N.G.: Nenagh Guardian; N.E.: Newry Examiner; N.T.:

Newry Telegraph; N.W.: Northern
Whig; R.G.: Roscommon Gazette;
S.C.: Sligo Champion; S.J.: Sligo
Journal; S.O.C.: Story of Comber;
T.B.W.: The Big Wind; T.A.:
Thom's Annals; T.C.: Tipperary
Constitution; T.F.P.: Tipperary
Free Press; T.H.: Tuam Herald;
T.O.M.: Tales of Mourne; T.M.:
Tralee Mercury; U.T.: Ulster
Times; W.C: Waterford Chronicle;
W.M.: Waterford Mail; W.C.:
Wexford Conservative; W.I.:
Wexford Independent.

Notes

1. *Dublin Evening Post*, January 8, 1839.
2. *Ballyshannon Herald*, quoting *Drogheda Journal* Jan. 19.
3. Thomas, *Man and the Natural World*, p30, 165.
4. Particularly in N. Ulster and S. Leinster; Danaher, *The Year in Ireland*. One form of this ran as follows: 'A fortnight before the Twelfth Night rushes are gathered and hung to dry. On the Twelfth day they are dipped in fat or gravy and let dry. Cow manure is shaped into a pancake and the rush candles stuck in. They are then named after living members of the family, and the first candle to die is the first of the family who will also die. In some places... the rosary is said while they burn.' DIF MSS Recorded off Thomas Brennan, 91, Creggs Co. Galway. Related lore abounds.
5. *Irish Geography*, 22, 1989, p38.
6. *Belfast News Letter*, Jan. 8; *Irish Book Lover* XVIII, 1930, p77: O'Donovan writes that in the Wicklow mountains the snow fell in 'luxuriant heavy drops'.
7. *Ulster Times*, Jan. 10; *Derry Journal*, Feb. 1929; T.O. Russell's recollections of the Big Wind of 1839, undated cutting (probably c. 1910) in the possession of Pat Gallagher, Bonniconlon, Ballina, Co Mayo. The cutting was kept in the family bible.
8. Cathal Dallat states that 'It was customary to have a huge barn brack made specially for this occasion'; *Seasonal Customs*. See also R.H. Buchanan, same volume. Epiphany is a public holiday in four EC countries.
9. *Limerick Chronicle*, Jan. 9.
10. *Irish Geography*, 22, 1989, p41.
11. *Dublin Evening Post*, Jan. 10, quoting *Kilkenny Journal*.
12. *Drogheda Journal*, Jan. 12.
13. *Galway Patriot*, Jan. 9.
14. *Catholic Bulletin*, Vol. 2, 1912, p16. The storms of 1839 and 1842 have this effect in common. Joyce's characterisation is too good to omit!

15.   *The Liberator*, Jan. 22; *Londonderry Journal*, Jan. 15.
16.   *Dublin Evening Post*, Jan. 8.
17.   *Irish Book Lover*, XVIII, 1930, p78.
18.   *Galway Weekly Advertiser*, Jan. 19.
19.   *Northern Whig*, Jan. 10.
20.   *Impartial Reporter*, Jan. 17, quoting *Dublin Evening Mail*.
21.   DIF SCH MSS Vol. 257, p170-1.
22.   *Dublin Evening Post*, Jan. 10, quoting *Kilkenny Journal*.
23.   *Derry Journal*, Feb., 1929
24.   *Kerry Evening Post*, Jan. 12.
25.   *Limerick Chronicle*, Jan. 9. Espy also mentions lightning in Glasgow, and the *Nautical Magazine and Naval Chronicle* records it in Liverpool.
26.   *Dublin Evening Post*, Jan. 8; MacDonagh papers *Donegal Annual*, Vol. 4 (3), 1960, p201: Shields & Fitzgerald, p33, are not convinced.
27.   *Drogheda Conservative Journal*, Jan. 12.
28.   *Dublin Evening Post*, Jan. 8. Artillary were placed to take out linking buildings, an exercise which turned into a fiasco when the officer in charge felt unable to order his men to fire (these were the houses of some of the city's leading professionals.) Authority was sent for, and as paralysis gripped the decision-making structure, the windward side of the block burned down, two gunners being killed or severely injured (accounts differ) by falling masonry.
29.   *Ibid.*, Jan. 10.
30.   Liam Cox, Church St., Moate, letter to author.
31.   *The Ulster Review*, Nov 1924, p131.
32.   *Ibid.; Dublin Evening Post*, Jan. 10.
33.   *Ibid.*
34.   It is difficult to gauge the effectiveness of the police response. Information is patchy, and the newspapers tended to print what suited them, for instance the nationalist *Galway Patriot* criticises their inactivity at Loughrea, whilst the tory *Kerry Evening Post* offers its constituency feelgood material like the story of the police making an heroic if slightly Keystone Cops-like chase through bog and morass to put out a fire. No contingency plans existed for this kind of emergency.
35.   *Thom's Annals of old Dublin*.
36.   *Limerick Chronicle*, Jan. 9.
37.   *Londonderry Journal*, Jan. 8.
38.   *Belfast News Letter*, Jan. 15.
39.   *Irish Book Lover*, XVIII, 1930, p78.
40.   *Ibid.*
41.   'When people were going to build a house they would at night put a sally rod in each of its would-be corners. If any of the sticks were knocked they would not build there as it would be on a "Fairy's Pass", and to build there would bring bad luck all their lives.' DIF SCH MSS Vol. 694, p265-6. This is one of many versions of this custom.
42.   DIF MSS Peter Cloonan, Craughwell, Co. Galway.

43. DIF MSS Mary Kettle, Cohan, Co. Cavan. The responses to the Poor Inquiry (1836) vividly demonstrate just how poor much of the rural housing stock was.
44. DIF SCH MSS Vol. 734, p245.
45. DIF MSS Peter Cloonan.
46. DIF MSS Mary Kettle.
47. *Northern Standard*, June 1, 1934.
48. *History of Doocastle*, p6. Drowning: DIF SCH MSS Vol. 257, p170-1; *Impartial Reporter* Jan. 17.
49. *Irish Geography*, 22, 1989, p38.
50. DIF SCH MSS Vol. 211, p143.
51. Ibid., p176.
52. *Béaloideas*, X, p96-8.
53. *Limerick Chronicle*, Jan. 16; *Northern Standard*, June 1 1934.
54. *Mayo Constitution*, Jan. 22, quoting *Newry Telegraph*.
55. *Biatas*, 17 (5), 1963, p314.
56. *The Mayo Constitution*, Jan. 22, mentions 'Large hay ricks containing from ten to fifteen tons'. As a glance at a photograph of any turn of the century stackyard will show, these massive hay boats were well and beautifully made.
57. Diary of Robert Dunlop, courtesy of David Dunlop, Portaferry.
58. *Journal Upper Ards Historical Society*, 7, 1983, p23.
59. *Kerry Evening Post*, Jan. 12.
60. *Northern Whig*, Jan. 15.
61. *Ibid.*, Jan. 8.
62. *Drogheda Conservative Journal*, Jan. 12.
63. NLI MS 3579-80.
64. *Catholic Bulletin*, Vol. 2, 1912, p15.
65. *Tuam Herald*, Jan. 19.
66. *The Liberator*, Jan. 22.
67. *Leinster Independent*, Jan. 12.
68. *Ibid.*
69. *Drogheda Journal*, Jan. 19.
70. *Northern Whig*, Jan. 15; *Impartial Reporte*r, Jan. 17; *Galway Weekly Advertiser*, Jan. 12.
71. *Catholic Bulletin*, Vol. 2, 1912, p15.
72. DIF SCH MSS Vol. 257, p170-1; *Drogheda Journal*, Jan. 19.
73. *Catholic Bulletin*, Vol. 2, 1912, p15.
74. *Waterford Chronicle*, Jan. 17.
75. Brian Dempsey, Ballykeeran, Athlone, letter to author.
76. McCracken, *Irish Woods since Tudor Times*, p140. The attitudes described here are well expressed by Dr Astrov in Chekov's *Uncle Vanya* (1897).
77. *Dublin Evening Post*, Jan. 15.
78. We should be wary of overestimating the extent to which the country was denuded. In 1841, Ireland had 345,000 acres under woodland,

however this figure would have included saplings, and can also be read as a tribute to the resilience of the country estate, and to the extensiveness of the replanting that followed the storm.

79. *Catholic Bulletin*, Vol. 2, 1912, p15.
80. *Northern Whig*, Jan. 15.
81. DIF MSS Vol. 257, p169.
82. *Béaloideas*, X, p96-8.
83. *Catholic Bulletin*, Vol. 2, 1912, p15.
84. DIF SCH MSS Vol. 257, p169-71.
85. DIF SCH MSS Vol. 211, p419-20; Vol. 211, p476; *Béaloideas*, X, p96-8.
86. *Drogheda Journal*, Jan. 15; DIF MSS Mrs Griffin, Ballymoe, Co. Galway; *Drogheda Conservative Journal*, Jan. 12.
87. DIF MSS Charles McCabe, Ballyglunin, Co. Galway.
88. DIF SCH MSS Vol 252, p87.
89. Colin Johnston Robb.
90. *Tralee Mercury*, Jan. 23.
91. DIF MSS Mary Kettle.
92. *Ibid.*
93. *Ibid.*
94. *Catholic Bulletin*, Vol. 2, 1912, p15.
95. DIF MSS Mary Kettle.
96. *Ulster Times*, Jan 12.
97. *Mayo Constitution*, Jan 15.
98. *Galway Weekly Advertiser*, Jan 19.
99. *Tipperary Constitution*, Jan. 22, quoting *Liverpool Mail*.
100. *Dublin Evening Post*, Jan. 10.
101. *Londonderry Sentinel,* Jan 26; *Journal Upper Ards Historical Society*, 7, 1983, p23; Nevin, *The Story of Comber*.
102. *Northern Whig*, Jan. 8.
103. *Ibid.*, Jan. 15.
104. *Ibid.*
105. *Waterford Chronicle*, Jan. 17.
106. *Ibid.*
107. *Drogheda Journal*, Jan. 8. There was also relief work, but it was short lived and indifferently paid.
108. Mary M'Veigh, Lr. Clonard Street, Belfast, letter to author.
109. *Leinster Independent*, Jan 12.
110. Insurance then meant mercantile, fire, or life cover only. Had modern 'weather peril' insurance been as widespread then as now the storm could conceivably have triggered an industry crash, with potentially dire knock-on effects for the whole financial sector. As it was insurers had to indemnify a relatively small circle of shipowners and assorted proprietors.
111. *Tuam Herald*, Jan. 19. The press were also greatly amused by 'A mad theorist, named Starling', who suggested that the earth should be seen

as a living animal, or in modern jargon, a self-regulating system, an idea rather like James Lovelock's currently fashionable 'Gaia'.

112. *Drogheda Journal*, Jan. 19, quoting *Londonderry Journal*.
113. *Impartial Reporter*, Jan. 17.
114. *Clonmel Herald*, Jan. 9, quoting *Cork Constitution*.
115. *Galway Weekly Advertiser*, Jan. 12.
116. *An Gaodhal*, 11 (3), p25-7.
117. *Béaloideas*, X, p96-8.
118. *Mayo Constitution*, Jan. 15.
119. *Ibid*.
120. *Ibid*.
121. *Limerick Chronicle*, Jan. 9.
122. *Downpatrick Recorder*, Jan. 12.
123. *Drogheda Journal*, Jan. 12.
124. *Tuam Herald*, Feb 23.
125. *Galway Patriot*, Jan. 16. Lady Clanrickarde gave a further £60 in cash and kind. The Marquis was then in Russia.
126. *Tralee Mercury*, Jan. 16.
127. *Galway Patriot*, Jan. 23.
128. *Drogheda Conservative Journal*, Jan. 19.
129. *Downpatrick Recorder*, Jan. 19.
130. *Drogheda Conservative Journal*, Jan. 12.
131. *Waterford Chronicle*, Jan 17.
132. *Kerry Evening Post*, Jan. 12.
133. *Drogheda Conservative Journal*, Jan. 19.
134. *Clonmel Herald*, Jan. 23.
135. *Galway Patriot*, Jan. 23.
136. *Ibid*.
137. *Tuam Herald*, Jan. 19, quoting *The Pilot*.
138. *Derry Journal*, Feb. 1929. The levy that paid for the workhouses syphoned off money from the numerous voluntary organisations that were then active in the field of relief. Catherine McAuley, founder of the Sisters of Mercy, a body which sought to support people in their own homes without institutionalising them, wrote bitterly deploring the tax. *The Correspondence of Catherine McAuley, 1827-1841*.
139. *Drogheda Journal*, Jan. 12.
140. Foster, *Modern Ireland*, p374.
141. *Biatas*, p310. Dr. John Watson, Medical Superintendent of Gransha Asylum, Derry, from 1914 on, dated patients according to whether or not they were alive at the time of the Big Wind of 1839.
142. *Downshire Chronicle*, Feb. 2.
143. *Dublin Historical Record*, Vol. XV (3), p66. Most of the other storm namings seem to be localised.
144. *Ibid*., quoting Rutty, who recorded over a hundred storms between 1716-65, few of which were bad, and none 'great'.
145. Whipple, *Storm*, p70-83.

146. *Ibid.; Irish Geography*, 22, 1989, p38-42; Lamb, *Historic Storms of the North Sea, etc.*, p131-33. Both accounts tally.

147. *Irish Geography*, 22, 1989, p38, quoting *Kerry Evening Post*, Jan. 12.

148. DIF MSS Mary Kettle. The fairies had been raising storms since the time of St. Patrick. When the saint told them that they would never see the light of heaven the fairy host 'raised a terrible storm and devastated the entire country'. Logan, *The Old Gods*, p17.

149. p4.

150. Rowley, *The Big Wind*, in *Tales of Mourne Country*.

151. Roy Johnston, pers. comm. These took place in King Street, where the Anacreontic Society had rooms. They performed the 1st symphony on Dec. 21st, 1837, and again on Jan. 4th 1838. Emboldened by what must have been their success they attempted the 2nd symphony on March 3rd. The 'Eroica' however, was probably beyond them, and would have had to wait.

152. DIF SCH MSS Vol. 255, p150-2.

153. As some medical authorities speculated that the human body could collapse during train travel if the engine exceeded 30 mph, who is to say who had the monopoly on the truth?

154. *Impartial Reporter* (transcribed) Jan. 17.

155. *Limerick Chronicle*, Jan. 12.

156. *Ibid.*

157. *Drogheda Conservative Journal*, Jan. 26.

158. *Londonderry Sentinel*, Jan. 19. The clerical response to the storm must also have been quite formidable. One can imagine storm texts being preached all over the country over the next few weeks, to the accompaniment of much brimstone. And what self-respecting clergyman would pass the chance over? At least one of these storm-derived sermons was published in pamphlet form in Belfast. *Downshire Chronicle*, Feb.2. By way of contrast, Irish science managed only a fairly muted response. Goaded by press criticism of its inactivity, the Royal Dublin Society attempted to assess its impact on the country's plantations; and the Statistical Society of Ulster, a little more ambitiously, attempted to gather and collate such barometric detail as had been recorded, towards a clearer understanding of the storm. *Dublin Evening Post*, Jan. 19; *Downshire Chronicle*, Feb. 2.

159. *An Gaodhal*, 11 (3), p25-7.

160. The Rosses, Co. Donegal *Donegal Annual*, Vol. 4 (3), 1960, p202; Dungannon, Co. Tyrone, after a man named Montgomery, hanged 'on the date' for murder (John McBride, Cabragh, letter to author); Derrygonnelly, Co. Fermanagh (Willie Parke, Drumary, Co. Fermanagh, letter to author); *The Spectator*, Feb. 25, 1939.

161. It was also capable of endowing enchantment. In Cork babies born during the storm (and they seem to have been induced in their hundreds!) were held to be charmed: 'it was believed that they would not leave [the earth] without doing some miracle'. DIF SCH MSS Vol 353, p236.

162. They were still being told. As one child in Roscommon put it: 'During the Winter nights my father often tells us all the stories he heard about the Big Wind of 1839'. DIF SCH MSS Vol. 257, p170-1.

163. O'Brien, *The Poor Mouth*, p69.

164. DIF MSS Tuam, Co. Galway.

165. This in spite of the founding of reading rooms by an odd mixture of religious and radical societies. Subs were renewed every January, and much effort was devoted to getting money out of 'delinquent subscribers' *Tipperary Constitution*, Jan. 8.

166. Most of these papers had relatively shallow roots in their communities and most had poor correspondent networks.

167. God too, probably had grounds for sending a stiff letter to the nineteenth century equivalent of the Press Council. He gets saddled with the responsiblity for sending the storm, emerging as a fairly alarming sort of character, while 'Providence' gets most of the credit for keeping people safe.

168. This can be confusing. Drogheda, for example, is described both as 'a complete wreck' and 'comparatively unscathed' in consecutive editions of the same paper. (*Drogheda Journal*, Jan. 8, Jan. 12.) The high price of labour suggests that there may have been more in the first assessment.

169. Egan, *Drumhome*, p41.

170. DIF MSS Charles McCabe, Ballyglunin, Co. Galway.

171. Egan, *Drumhome*, p41. It may have affected small-scale protective planting: 'Immediately after [1839] people started to plant on the stormy side of their house. They went back about 6ft and they planted trees... which, a generation later became a real menace to the house which they overhung.' *History of Doocastle, Co. Sligo*, p6.

172. *Irish Geography*, 22, 1989, p38, quoting *Seanchas Thomáis Laighléis*, p61.

173. *Irish Geography*, 22, 1989, p38.

Bibliography

1. Manuscripts

DIF MSS (Manuscripts held in the Department of Irish Folklore, University College Dublin: Vol. 172, p143; Vol. 279; Vol. 463, p25; Vol. 485, p271-2; Vol. 732, p435-6; Vol. 815, p144-5; Vol. 1040, p677-8; Vol. 1356, p104-11; Vol. 1364, p354; Vol. 1839, p285-6.

DIF SCH MSS (Schools Project Manuscripts): Vol. 14, p343; Vol. 16; Vol. 21; Vol. 211, ps143, 147, 176-9, 419-20; Vol. 248; Vol. 252, p87; Vol. 255, p150-2; Vol. 257, ps169, 170-1, 268; Vol. 353, p12; Vol. 734, p245.

Dunlop, Robert (b.1825, in Clough Co. Antrim): diary.

Howard, Mrs. Francis: diary, N.L.I. MSS 3579-80.

Johnston, Roy: Untitled Phd. thesis (in preparation).

Nevin, Norman *The Story of Comber*, Comber Library.

Pilson, Aynesworth *A Downpatrick Diary 1799-1849*, P.R.O.N.I. D365/3.

Stronaghan, Sam (of Spamount, Co. Down): tape, recorded by Arthur Davidson, Ballynahinch.

2. Contemporary newspapers

Belfast News Letter, Clonmel Herald, Downpatrick Recorder, Downshire Chronicle, Drogheda Conservative Journal, Drogheda Journal, Dublin Evening Mail, Dublin Evening Post, Galway Patriot, Galway Weekly Advertiser, Impartial Reporter, Kerry Evening Post, Leinster Independent, Liberator, Limerick Chronicle, Londonderry Journal, Londonderry Sentinel, Mayo Constitution, Northern Whig, Tipperary Constitution, Tipperary Free Press, Tralee Mercury, Tuam Herald, Ulster Times, Waterford Chronicle.

3. Articles

Béaloideas X, p96-8.

Bowes, Leo *The Night of the Big Wind, Ireland's Own*, Jan. 9, 1987, p32.

Buchanan, R.H.; Dallat, Cathal in *Seasonal Customs*, Ulster Folklife Studies (Coleraine, 1988)

Burke, M. *An Gaodhal*, 11 (3), 1895, p25-7.

Burt, S.D. *A new north Atlantic low pressure record, Weather*, 42 (2), 1987, p53-6.

Carolan, Nicholas 'Here's good health to Asquith': songs on the old age pension, Ceol Tíre, March 1981, p12-16.

Clow, D.G. *Daniel Defoe's account of the storm of 1703, Weather*, 43 (3), 1988, p140-1.

Danaher, Kevin *The Night of the Big Wind, Biatas*, 17 (5), 1963, p311-15.

Derry Journal, The Night of the Big Wind, undated cutting, Feb.? 1929.

Dixon, F.E. *Weather in Old Dublin, Dublin Historical Record*, 15, 1989, p65-72.

Donegal Annual, The Night of the Big Wind in County Donegal (MS account, Vol 4, no 3, 1960, p201-3.

Irish Book Lover, The Night of the Big Wind, Vol. XVIII, No. 3, May-June 1930, p77-9.

Irish Builder, Ireland after the recent Gale, 44, Mar. 26 1903, p1656-8.

Irish Independent, Jan. 4, 1939, p5; Jan. 6, p5.

Irish Monthly, The Poet and the Painter: an episode in the Night of the Big Wind, Vol. XIX, 1891, p428-34.

Joyce, P.W. *Recollections of Two Great Storms, Irish Catholic Bulletin*, Vol. 2, 1912, p15-16.

Lamb, H.H. *The storm of 15-16 October 1987: historical perspective, Weather*, 43 (3), 1988, p136-9.

Leslie, Shane, *A Wreath of Folklore, The Ulster Review*, Vol. 1, No. 6, Nov. 1924, p131.

McDonough, Michael O. *The Night of the Big Wind, Journal of the Old Drogheda Society*, Vol. 7, 1990, p5-12.

Moore, John *The Big Wind, The Spectator*, Feb. 25, 1939.

MacRory, Colin *The Night of the Big Wind, Irish Weekly*, Aug.? 1974, p5-12.

Northern Standard, The Night of the Big Wind, Rockcorry resident's account, June 1, 1934.

O'Casaide, P. *A noted family of Greaghnarogue, Macalla*, 1976-9, p20-22.

Patton, Jim *The Big Wind of 150 Years Ago, East Belfast Post*, Aug. 24, 1989, p6.

Quine, C.P. *Damage to trees and woodlands in the storm of 15-16 October 1987, Weather*, 43 (3), 1988, p114-8.

Rutherford, J.C. *Life of Rev. John Orr*, Part II, *Journal of the Upper Ards Historical Society*, Vol. 7, 1983, p23.

Shield, Lisa, & Fitzgerald, Denis *The Night of the Big Wind in Ireland, 6-7 January, 1839; Irish Geography* Vol. 22, 1989, p31-43.

4. Books

Anderson, William *Original Poems* (Belfast, 1861)

Barrow, G.L. *The Emergence of the Irish Banking System* (Dublin, 1975)

Bettelheim, Bruno *The Uses of Enchantment: the meaning and importance of fairy tales* (London, 1976)

Beckett, J.C. *The Making of Modern Ireland 1603-1923* (London, 1966)

Bolster, Angela (ed) *The Correspondence of Catherine McAuley 1827-1841* (Dublin, 1988)

Boydell, B. (ed) *Four Centuries of Music in Ireland* (London, 1979)

Brownas, Geoffrey *Japanese Rainmaking* (London, 1963)

Cockerell, H.A.L., & Green, Edwin *The British Insurance Business 1547-1970* (London, 1976)

Coogan, Beatrice *The Big Wind* (London, 1969)

Danaher, Kevin *The Year in Ireland* (Cork, 1972)

Donaldson, Dixon *History of Islandmagee* (1927)

Dublin Almanac & General Register of Ireland 1835 (Dublin, 1834)

Dublin Almanac & General Register of Ireland 1842 (Dublin, 1841)

Egan, Bernard *Drumhome* (Donegal, 1986)

Espy, J.P. *The Philosophy of Storms* (Boston, 1841)

Evans, E.E. *Irish Heritage: the landscape, the people and their work* (Dundalk, 1942)

Evans, E.E. *Irish Folk Ways* (London, 1957)

Foster, R.F. *Modern Ireland 1600-1972* (London, 1988)

Freeman, T.W. *Pre-Famine Ireland: a study in historical geography* (London 1957)

Green, Miranda *The Gods of the Celts* (Gloucester, 1986)

Green, Victor, J. *Festivals & Saints' Days* (Poole, 1978)

Hanna, A *These Three hundred and forty years of Witness* (Dundonald, 1985)

Lamb, Hubert *Historic Storms of the North Sea, British Isles and Northwest Europe* (Cambridge, 1991)

Laughton, C. & Heddon, V. *Great Storms* (London, 1927)

Lefroy, Paul *Memoir of Chief Justice Lefroy* (unknown)

Logan, Patrick *Irish Country Cures* (Belfast, 1981)

Logan, Patrick *The Old Gods: the Facts about Irish Fairies* (Belfast, 1981)

McConnon, M.P. *Castlebellingham* (Castlebellingham, unknown)

McCracken, Eileen *Irish Woods since Tudor Times: their Distribution and Exploitation* (Belfast, 1971)

Maguire, W.A. *The Downshire Estates in Ireland 1801-1845* (Oxford, 1972)

Mason, A. *The Wee Men of Ballywooden* (unknown, 1930)

Matthews, Caitlin *The Celtic Tradition* (Dorset, 1989)

O'Brien, Flann *The Poor Mouth* (London, 1975)

O'Farrell, Padraic *Superstitions of the Irish Country People* (Cork, 1978)

Rowley, Richard *Tales of Mourne* (Bristol, 1937)

Simpson, Noel *The Belfast Bank 1827-1970* (Belfast, 1975)
Supple, B.E. *The Royal Exchange Assurance: a History of British Insurance 1720-1970* (Cambridge, 1970)
Thomas, Keith *Man and the Natural World* (London, 1983)
Whipple, A.B.C. *Storm* (Amsterdam, 1982)
Thom's Annals of Old Dublin (Dublin, 1927)
Wilde, Lady *Quaint Irish Customs and Superstitions* (Dublin, 1988)
Wilson, Ian *Shipwrecks of the Ulster Coast* (Coleraine,1979)
Witherow, Thomas *The Autobiography of Thomas Witherow (1824-1890)* (Draperstown, 1990)
Wood-Martin, W.G. *Traces of the Elder Faiths of Ireland* (London, 1902)

Index

Achill 50
Andrew Nugent, the 39, 50, 73
Animals 26-7, 31, 44, 73, 80, 83, 87, 98, 100, 104, 105, 109, 112, 121
Annadale 70
Antrim, County 27, 64, 67, 68, 74, 91, 94, 103, 114
Antiquities 32, 74, 89, 104, 111, 118, 119
Ardee 64
Ardglass 65
Armagh 65; County 106, 107, 113; Observatory 55
Aran Islands 64
Arson 72
Asquith 57
Athlone 21, 28, 30, 65-6
Atlantic Ocean 16, 29, 32, 48
Aughnacloy 67
Aurora borealis 20, 35

Balbriggan 36-7, 66
Ballina 98
Ballinasloe 29, 41, 67
Ballybofey 118
Ballycastle 94
Ballygawley 67
Ballylesson 28
Ballymena 67
Ballynahinch 68, 107
Ballyshanon 68
Bandon 117
Bangor 68
Bantry 117
Beethoven 48
Belfast 16, 20, 28, 29, 36, 37, 39, 65, 68-71, 95, 108
Belvoir 70
Birr 71
Blarney 28, 71
Booth, Robert Gore 104
Borrisokane 71

Boyle 71-2
Boyne, River 32, 117
Bray 72
Breweries 71, 85, 87, 120
Brighton 41
Bruff 20, 72
Buncrana 72
Bundoran 73
Bunratty 91
Burke, Michael 39, 50
Burtonport 39, 73

Caherguillamore 73
Caledon 73
Canals 14, 96; Grand Canal 23, 87; Canal Company 96
Cappagh 64, 73
Carlow 37, 73-4
Carnmore 74
Carrickfergus 74
Carrickmacross 29
Carrick-on-Shannon 75
Carrick-on-Suir 75
Cashel 75
Castlebar 65-6
Castlebellingham 76
Castlecoole 76, 92
Castle Forbes 76
Castleknock 87
Castlepollard 77
Castlereagh 70
Cavan 77-8; County 28, 33, 100
Chimneys, factory 35, 36, 68, 69-70, 79, 90, 98, 99; domestic 19, 38, 74, 80, 98, 102, 103, 118, 120
Churches 21, 35, 65, 83, 84, 91, 98, 99, 101, 103, 105, 107, 111, 115, 118, 121; the burning of Bethesda 20, 88
Clancarty, earl of 29, 41, 67
Clare, County 25, 26, 91, 97, 100, 111, 121
Clifden 78

Clonakilty 78, 117
Clones 78
Clonmel 78
Clough (Co. Antrim) 27
Clough (Co. Down) 78
Cloughey 114
Coastguard 94, 115, 116
Cobh 15, 44, 79
Comber 79
Convoy 79
Cookstown 79-80
Coolany 80
Cootehill 78
Cork 38, 63, 71, 79-81; County 32, 33, 48, 78-9, 92, 101, 108, 116, 117
Creeve 81
Crehan, 'Junior' 26
Crawfordsburn 68
Crumlin (Co. Dublin) 87
Crossgar 81
Crossmolina 81
Cultra 95

Danaher, Kevin 52
Darney 81
Death(s) 23, 38-9, 66, 68, 69, 70, 71, 80, 81, 85, 86, 92, 95, 100, 105, 109, 112, 115, 116, 117, 121, 122; coffins exhumed 28; divination 14; body divining 48; wakes 28
Defoe, Daniel 47, 50
Denmark 47
Derry/Londonderry 81-2; County 45, 83, 84, 102, 108
Derrygonnelly 82
Devil(s) 48, 93
Diligence, the 39, 94
Dingle 82
Disraeli 44
Distilleries 69, 74, 85, 87, 92, 121
Donaghadee 50, 82-3
Donaghmore 83
Donegal 83; County 29, 50, 68, 72, 73, 74, 79, 81, 82, 83, 85, 90, 94, 95, 99, 101, 114, 115, 116, 118
Donnybrook 87

Down, County 29, 32, 65, 68, 78, 79, 81, 83, 90, 96, 99, 100, 101, 112, 113, 115, 116, 122
Downhill 83
Downpatrick 83-4
Draperstown 84
Drogheda 18, 35, 37, 41, 42-4, 65, 84-5
Dromara 85
Dromena 97
Dromore 85-6
Drumbo 71
Drumlish 86
Drumsna 86
Dublin 18, 20, 22, 30, 31, 35, 53, 63, 86-9; Castle 35; County 66, 108, 117
Dufferin, Lord 68
Duleek 89
Dun Laoghaire 89
Dundalk 35, 90
Dundrum 90
Dunkineely 90
Dunleer 90
Dunmurry 91

Edgeworthstown 91
England 37, 47
Ennis 91
Enniskillen 91
Epiphany 13, 14
Esker 50, 66
Espy, James 37

Factories 18, 35, 36, 68, 69-70, 85
Famine, the great 46, 51, 58; fears of 44
Fairy belief 48-9, 97
Fermanagh, County 50, 76, 82, 91
Finnea 92
Fire: burning houses 21, 22, 66, 76, 78, 81, 96, 104, 106, 108-9, 110, 111, 121; domestic 22; fighting 21, 22, 37, 88, 97
Fish 22, 31, 39
Flooding 22, 23, 105, 118; torrential rain 23; lake agitated 97
Foaty 92
Forges 108

Freemasonry 48
Furnishings: beds and bedding 18, 19,
33, 38, 72, 107; stools 33; delft 16;
pots and pans 33

Galway 18, 38, 42, 44, 93-4; County 22,
27, 28, 39, 50, 64, 67, 78, 92, 96,
106, 113, 116, 118, 120
Gentry 29-31, 41-2, 65, 77, 101, 118;
absentee 41, 42
Giant's Causeway 39, 63, 94
Glasgow 71
Glasnevin 87
Glenarm 94
God 13, 32, 118; storm God-given 49,
52, 92, 93
Gort 94
Government, role of 41
Granard 94-5
Greyabbey 95

Hebrides 47
Hillsborough 95
Holywood 68, 71, 95
Housing 18, 24, 36, 37, 46, 55, 69, 89,
97, 102, 108, 111, 112, 117
Howard, Mrs. Francis 16, 28, 29

Insurance 37
Irish Sea 32, 39
Island Magee 28, 95

Japan 49
Joyce, P.W. 29, 32
Judgement, Day of 14
Julianstown 95-6

Kanturk 32
Kearney 114
Kells 96
Kerry, County 48, 67, 82, 96, 98, 104,
118, 119
Kilbeggan 16, 20, 21, 96
Kildare, County 110
Killala 39-40, 98
Kilconnell 96

Kilgory 92, 97
Kilkee 97
Kilkenny 97-8
Killarney 98, 113
Killough 71, 99
Killinchy 114
Killybegs 39, 99
Killyleagh 99
Kilmore 100
Kingscourt 78, 100
Kinsale 101
Kircubbin 101

Lanesborough 101
Laighléis, Tomás 56
Larne Lough 95
Laois, County 101, 108, 109, 114
Lefroy, Thomas 30
Leitrim, County 25, 26, 27, 75, 86
Letterkenny 101
Lifford 101
Lightning 18
Limavady 102
Limerick 16, 17, 22, 37, 40, 63, 102-3;
County 20, 27, 72, 73, 80
Lisburn 103
Lissadell 104
Little Christmas 14, 15
Liverpool 39, 41, 89
London, Great Fire of 21; Lloyds of 114
Londonderry: see Derry
Longford 19, 30, 38, 105; County 67,
76, 86, 91, 101
Looting 34-5, 39, 107, 119
Loughgall 106
Loyghrea 21, 35, 106-7
Louth, County 64, 76, 79, 84, 90, 119
Lurgan 107

Magherafelt 108
Malahide 108
Manchester 36, 41
Mansions/large houses 29, 92, 95, 107,
115, 118
Maralin 122
Maryborough 108

Mayo, County 29, 40, 74, 75, 81, 118
Meath, County 89, 95, 110, 117, 120
Menai Bridge 47
Moate 22, 25, 96, 108-9
Moira 107
Monaghan 109; County 22, 25, 27, 78, 81
Moneyrea 71
Mountjoy, Lady 19
Mourne Mountains 48
Mullingar 109-110
Mountmellick 109
Munro, Henry 107

Naas 110
Navan 110
Nenagh 34, 111
Newcastle (Co. Down) 111
Newcastle (Co. Wicklow) 111
Newgrove 27, 111
Newry 29, 112
Newspapers: promoting giving 42-3; storm reporting 49, 53-55; character of 53-5
Newtownards 112
Newtown Forbes 30, 31
New York 39
North Sea 47

O'Brien, Flann 51
O'Connell, Daniel 42, 52
O'Donovan, John 18
Offaly, County 34, 71, 78, 101, 113, 121
Omagh 112
Ordnance Survey 113
Oughterard 113

Pallas 113
Pensions Act 59
Philipstown 113
Phoenix Park 16, 30
Police, response to storm 22, 66, 89, 96, 104
'Poor', the: urban 18, 36, 41, 44, 54, 87, 91, 102, 106; rural 26, 35, 44, 54-5, 63, 82, 93, 99, 112, 120

Poor Law 41-2, 55, 63, 94
Portadown 18, 113
Portaferry 28, 113-4
Portarlington 114
Portpatrick 83
Portrush 114
Powerscourt 72, 123
Protestantism 34, 43, 53
Púca, the 48

Rathfarnham 87
Rathmullan 115
Randalstown 114
Raphoe 114-5
Rathfriland 115
Rathmines 87
Relief: 41-4, 76, 80; involvement of churches in 18, 42
Religious awakening 50-1
Roads 14, 29, 66, 75, 104, 108, 109, 123
Robinson, Thomas Romney 55
Romanticism 20, 97-8
Roofs 19, 24, 39, 98, 101, 105, 115, 122
Roscommon, County 31, 71, 115
Roscrea 34, 115
Ross 28, 116
Rossnowlagh 116
Roundstone 116
Rowley, Richard 48
Royal Dublin Society 64

Saintfield 116
Salthill 116
Schools Scheme 52
Scotland 37, 47
Seaforde 29, 116-7
Secret societies 35, 45
Shannon, River 23, 32, 66
Shields, Lisa & Fitzgerald, Denis 49
Shinrone 34
Shipping 14, 37, 39-40, 72, 73, 79, 82-3, 85, 89-90, 93, 94, 100, 101, 103, 114, 115, 116, 118, 123
Skerries 117
Skibbereen 117

Sligo 18, 117; County 80, 104, 109
Snow 14, 35, 89
Somerville, Sir William 67
Spiddal 118
Storms: causes 47; historical 46, 84,
    103, 119
Strabane 23, 118
Strangford Lough 28
Streamstown 110
Swinford 118
Swords 16

Tallaght 87
Tarbert 118-9
Thatch/ing 24, 37, 38, 41, 57, 111, 120,
    122
Thimblemen 35
Thurles 119
Tipperary, County 71, 75, 78, 109, 111,
    115, 119
Tone, Wolfe 46
Tralee 119-20
Trees 29-31, 63, 64, 67, 76, 77, 79, 84,
    95, 96, 98, 101, 110, 111, 116, 117
Trim 120
Tuam 120
Tullamore 23, 121
Twelfth Night 13, 14
Typhus 44
Tyrone, County 22, 50, 67, 73, 79, 112,
    118, 121

Ulster 35
Unemployment 36-7
Urlingford 75

Wales 47
Waterford 40, 122-3
Westmeath, County 16, 24, 65, 77, 92,
    96, 108, 113, 123
Westminster 57
Westport 98
Wexford 123; County 116
Whirlwinds 18, 48
Wicklow, County 72, 111, 123;
    Mountains 18

Wilde, Lady 18
Windmills 35, 68, 110, 114, 116
Wood-Martin, W.G. 48

Youghal 101

Blackmouth & Dissenter

John M. Barkley

Hbk, 192pp, illustrated, £12.95

In this engaging memoir, which will delight his admirers and offer his detractors no comfort, Dr. Barkley, 'without doubt one of the most influential Irish Churchmen of the second half of the twentieth century', writes of his life and the experiences that formed him, lacing his narrative with some astringent criticism of contemporary Irish Presbyterianism, and explaining why, if he were a young man today, he would have serious reservations about joining the Presbyterian Church.

"John Barkley, often regarded by others as a heretic, sees himself as the exponent of the central tradition of the Presbyterian Church in its truly reformed spirit, and an outspoken opponent of all tendencies to turn the church he loves so well into something like an 'evangelical sect'. But this is not a dry book about doctrinal controversies, it is a warm human story, with much humour and many anecdotes by a great ecumenical churchman who has often had to swim against the stream."

Corrymeela News

"An enthralling, delightful story covering a broad canvas of Irish Presbyterianism from Malin to Mallusk over eighty years. To those who have experienced Dr. Barkley's sparkling personality and his deep erudition, his personal observations and commentary on ecumenism and political dialogue will make compulsive reading and his life-story, a mini history of Ulster life, will be assured an enthusiastic welcome by his own church and many other denominationalists." *Derry Journal*

Two Centuries of Life in Down 1600-1800

John Stevenson

Pbk, 508pp, illustrated, £7.95

Pirates roaming the coast, clerics being paid in beer, shopkeepers issuing their own coinage, French and Spanish money in daily circulation, hanging a man for stealing a chisel... the County Down of several centuries ago reads more like something from the world of science fiction than the place we are familiar with today.

In **Two Centuries of Life in Down 1600-1800**, John Stevenson brings this forgotten world to life, familiarising us with its customs, tastes and values, and subtly drawing the reader into the lives of a wide variety of its people, from the drunken Viscount and the dowager with servant trouble, to the small farmer facing eviction.

No subject is too trivial for him. He is as happy discussing fashion, witchcraft, hospitality and folk cures, as the Kirk, Public Morals, or the dangers of reading Milton. The result is something of a tour de force, a book of vast range and daring, and one of the great landmarks of literary County Down.

"no dry-as-dust academic work this, but a wonderful source for local historians, and a marvellous read for anyone who is interested in County Down..."

W.A. Maguire, Keeper of Local History, Ulster Museum.

The Most Unpretending of Places

A History of Dundonald, County Down

Peter Carr

Pbk, 256pp, illustrated, £7.95

"Sparkles with compelling detail... one of the most impressive local histories available for any locality on this island, north or south."   *Linenhall Review*

"One word could suffice to describe this book, magnificent! ...I cannot praise it too highly. Well illustrated with photographs, studiously annotated without over-loading the text, a questioning of sources, a good index and the courage to express opinions of a controversial nature. This is what local history is all about."   *Irish News*

Yes Matron

A history of nurses and nursing at the Royal Victoria Hospital, Belfast

Peggy Donaldson

Hbk, 200pp, illustrated, £12.50

Drawing both on her own nursing experience and a rich vein of oral and archive material, Peggy Donaldson creates a fresh and readable narrative that will delight, surprise and be treasured by anyone with an interest in nursing.

"Examines both great events and small, from the impact of wars and devastating epidemics, to the dramas of everyday hospital life... a humorous, heartwarming, moving story."   *Belfast Telegraph*

Gape Row

Agnes Romilly White's classic comedy

Pbk, 200pp, £4.95

Can Jinanna escape the poorhouse? Will young Johnny Darragh jilt Ann? Will Mary get saddled with the awful Andy John McCready? Or will Happy Bill, the wayside preacher, nip in first and win them all for God?

A boisterous, rich, nostalgic book which immerses the reader in the cheerful chaos of everyday life in a small Irish village on the eve of the First World War.

"Captures the spirit of early twentieth century rural Ulster better than any painter of photographer could."   *Sunday News*

"masterly... the dialogue goes to one's head like wine."   *The Observer*

Available from bookshops, or directly from the publishers.
If ordering, please add £1 for postage and packaging.